SO YOU WANT TO BE
PRESIDENT?

JOHN WARNER

FIND OUT IF YOU HAVE THE EGO, BANKROLL, AND MORAL "FLEXIBILITY" TO LEAD THE NATION AND TAKE ON THE WORLD

TOW BOOKS

Cincinnati, Ohio
www.towbooks.com

12 11 10 09 08   5 4 3 2 1

Distributed in Canada by Fraser Direct, 100 Armstrong Avenue, Georgetown, ON, Canada L7G 5S4, Tel: (905) 877-4411; Distributed in the U.K. and Europe by David & Charles, Brunel House, Newton Abbot, Devon, TQ12 4PU, England, Tel: (+44) 1626 323200, Fax: (+44) 1626 323319, E-mail: postmaster@davidandcharles.co.uk; Distributed in Australia by Capricorn Link, P.O. Box 704, Windsor, NSW 2756 Australia, Tel: (02) 4577-3555

Library of Congress Cataloging-in-Publication Data

Warner, John.

   So you want to be President? : find out if you have the ego, bankroll, and moral "flexibility" to become the most powerful person in the world / by John Warner. -- 1st ed.

      p. cm.

   ISBN 978-1-58297-519-1 (pbk. : alk. paper)

   1. Presidents--United States--Election--Humor. I. Title.

   PN6231.P693W37 2008

   818'.602--dc22

                                                              2007047211

Edited by Jane Friedman
Cover and interior designed by Claudean Wheeler
Production coordinated by Mark Griffin

For Dad, who would've loved this.

TABLE OF CONTENTS

INTRODUCTION

So You Want to Be President?.. 1

THIS HEIGHT OR TALLER TO RUN 8
Are You Qualified to Be President?

BUT ARE YOU REALLY QUALIFIED?.. 14
How Much Baggage Are You Carrying?

ELEPHANT, DONKEY, OR SOME KIND OF ELEPHONKEY? 17
Your Place on the Political Spectrum

ARE YOU REALLY SURE YOU WANT TO BE PRESIDENT? 28
Plowing Past the Fail-Safe Point

THE PRIMARIES   32

ANNOUNCING YOUR CANDIDACY 34
Meeting Tim Russert

MONEY-MONEY-MONEY-MONEY ... MONEY! 46
You and Your Campaign Coffers

FRIEND OR FOE? 54
You and Your Special Interest Groups

SHAMELESS PANDERING IS NOT A FACTOR FOR YOU 56
Appealing to the Primary Voter

**SHAKING BABIES AND KISSING HANDS,
OR IS IT THE OTHER WAY AROUND?** 67
The Primary States

GENERAL ELECTION

TIME OUT FOR SOME FUN 82
You and Your Campaign Slogan

[INSERT YOUR NAME HERE] FOR PRESIDENT................................86
You and Your Logo

PLEASED TO MEET YOU ... AND YOU ... AND YOU 90
You and Your Handshake

SHIT YOU SHOULD PROBABLY KNOW: PART 1 98
The Constitution

I NOW DECLARE YOU RUNNING MATES..101
Choosing Your Vice President

THEY LIKE YOU ... THEY REALLY, REALLY LIKE YOU! 108
You and Your Nominating Convention

I CAN NAME THAT BLOWHARD IN THREE ... NO, TWO PHRASES............112
You and the Media Personalities

THE DIRT OF YOUR ENEMY IS YOUR VICTORY SOAP......................119
You and Opposition Research

YOU DIDN'T DO ALL THAT YOURSELF, DID YOU? 123
You Are Not a Crook (But Your Cronies Should Be)

SHIT YOU SHOULD PROBABLY KNOW, PART II...............................124
The Concerns of Everyday People Who Are Nothing Like You

POLLING, POLLING, POLLING ... KEEP THOSE SURVEYS ROLLING 129
Public Opinion Polling

DODGE, BOB, AND WEAVE...137
The Third Rails of Politics

SORRY SEEMS TO BE THE HARDEST WORD..................................143
Cleaning Up Your Mistakes

ONE NATION UNDER GOD **147**
    You and Religion

SHIT YOU SHOULD KNOW, PART III **151**
    Foreign Relations

GO NEGATIVE OR GO HOME **157**
    You and Your Last, Best Hope

ELECTION DAY **167**

INTRODUCTION

So You Want to Be President?

Congratulations! By purchasing or even picking up this book,[1] you've indicated that you'd like to be president of the United States!

The cover blurb asks if you're ready to be the most powerful person in the world, but I just wrote that to get your attention. In truth, the president of the United States is only the second most powerful person in the world, behind Oprah.

Fortunately, as recent history—and indeed, all of history—has shown, *being* president isn't all that hard. Approval numbers lower than Michael Moore's scrotum in a 160-degree sauna aren't a problem once you're president. In fact, it's shockingly difficult to get booted from the Oval Office. If George W. Bush could start a war for no reason, Jimmy Carter could attempt to sell Louisiana to Iran in return for the hostages, and Woodrow Wilson could conduct international diplomacy by sending strippergrams extolling the virtues of the League of Nations to world leaders and still stay

---

[1] In picking up this book, you've probably already noticed that I've instructed my publisher to coat the cover with an ultra-tacky adhesive, thereby requiring you to either shoplift the book or pay for it. If the marketing guys have sprung for some space on a display table, it's possible that you're now holding an entire stack of books, each copy stuck to the next. Let me remind you that a criminal record will automatically disqualify you from becoming president of the United States. If this book isn't covered with an ultra-tacky adhesive, then you've likely read about my lawsuit against the publisher for refusing to agree to my totally reasonable demands. Either way, I'm rich now.

in office, I can't imagine what it would take to get removed as commander in chief.

Maybe getting oral sex from a White House intern. Maybe if you then lied about it. Maybe.

You're guaranteed *at least* four years as president (eight if you hire Karl Rove), no matter how badly you screw things up. Imagine if George W. Bush's performance as president were translated to any other job and how long *you'd* last:

- Despite repeated warnings from your Wendy's co-workers that boiling-hot grease will unleash sectarian violence on your flesh in the form of third-degree burns, you nonetheless plunge your entire arm into the deep fat fryer.

- After landing the morning zoo disc-jockey job in New York—following years of toil in markets like Yuma, Arizona, and West Gulch, New Mexico—acting out of loyalty, you hire your friend Alberto to be your sidekick, despite the fact that he communicates entirely via popping and clicking noises and banging the heel of his hand against his forehead.

- You're CEO of a large corporation, and the chief accountant comes into your office declaring that the company has hit record-setting debt levels that threaten to plunge it into a bottomless fiscal pit. Rather than figuring out how to tighten belts to get closer to solvency, you decide to give raises to the highest-paid employees and free vitamins to everyone over sixty.

- Your plumbing business offers twenty-four-hour emergency service, but when a desperate call comes in from a customer whose hot-water heater has exploded and caused a catastrophic flood in the basement that is threatening to engulf the entire house and ruin all the customer's possessions, you decide to wait a couple of days to see how things shake out before making the service call. When you finally do show up, you've brought the wrong tools and have to go back to the shop.

• As a trial attorney, during the most important case of your life, following jury selection, you fly an F-16 into the courtroom and declare victory.

• As the head of [insert any type of organization here], you allow your employees to fuck stuff up over and over and over again, yet you never fire them, and in some cases you promote them or give them medals.

If you think about it (and I have), there's only a handful of jobs more secure than being president of the United States:

SUPREME COURT JUSTICE: Appointed for life. Even when you're drooling into your oatmeal and consulting the Teletubbies on your opinions, you get to stay on the bench.

ITINERANT STRAWBERRY PICKER: Does a job Americans won't do.

TENURED PROFESSOR AT AN AMERICAN UNIVERSITY: The only firing offenses are having sex with a student in front of the class or voting Republican.

DUDE WHO LICKS THE COLOR OFF THE M&M'S BACKSTAGE AT THE AVRIL LAVIGNE CONCERT: Possesses a highly specialized skill.

UNION STEWARD FOR A GOVERNMENT AGENCY: Mess with the steward, mess with the union.[2]

Perhaps the better question than "So you want to be president?" is "Who *wouldn't* want to be president?" How about the perks?

---

[2] True story: I spent one summer working for a government agency that will remain nameless, but whose name rhymes with "Ghostal Pervis." The union steward, "Larry," despite spending his eight daily hours within the confines of the building, never did any actual labor. Every day, post-lunch, he would look through the pile of rhymes-with-"gail" that we'd be sorting, pluck out a couple of rhymes-with-"lagazines" (usually rhymes-with-"Smashonal Peographic," "Lopular Plechanics," and "Wayboy"), announce that he had to "go lay some wolf bait" and disappear into the can for the next couple of hours.

Nice house (rent-free), massive staff (taxpayer-supported), private plane (and helicopter, and hovercraft, and super-secret modes of transportation the public doesn't even know about[3]), guaranteed television exposure ... it's like being Donald Trump, except with your own hair, *and* access to nukes.

Sure, you stand a better chance of being assassinated than the average Joe. And you're going to get booed when you throw out the first pitch on baseball's opening day. But, dude, *you get to throw out the first pitch on opening day!* And I bet front-row tickets to the *American Idol* finale would totally be available too!

Plus, when you die, there's a parade!

That said, *becoming* president—*getting elected* president—is much, much harder than *being* president. Consider all the great historical figures who have never been elected President:

BOB DOLE	FLORIDA EVANS
WINSTON CHURCHILL	ANNE FRANK
LASSIE	Q*BERT
THOMAS JEFFERSON	

As you can deduce from this list, there's no real pattern to what might cause you to *not* become President. For example, the eminently qualified Bob Dole, a war hero with a lifetime of dedicated public service in the United States Senate, simply ran into an incumbent who was a superior campaigner and politician.[4] Anne Frank, on the other hand, was killed by Nazis. Lassie was disqualified from even running due to a controversy over how to calculate her age. (Is she 9, or 63?) Winston Churchill was actually a collie, and Q*Bert never could overcome his compulsion to speak only in profanities.

---

[3] I'm imagining some sort of pneumatic-tube system that runs under the Earth's crust, allowing the president to be transported to any other country at thousands of miles per hour using only air pressure.

[4] And who for sure didn't need a "little blue pill" for anything, if you catch my drift.

Another reason it's difficult to get elected president is that, to the unlearned, there appears to be no real formula to winning. Every campaign is *sui generis*,[5] each offering little insight as to what might work the next time around.

Take a look at these famous winning campaign strategies. Note the variety:

GEORGE WASHINGTON: War hero. Founded country. Had cool wooden teeth.

ABRAHAM LINCOLN: First candidate to run on "image." Capitalized on rail-splitting–honed pectorals in a series of bare-chested, beefcake campaign posters.

ZACHARY TAYLOR: Nobody remembers him or how he was elected president.

TEDDY ROOSEVELT: Appeal rested on resemblance to a cuddly stuffed toy.

AMELIA EARHART: Wasn't actually president.

HERBERT HOOVER: Exploiting a since-closed campaign loophole, exchanged chickens in pots and cars in garages for votes.

JOHN F. KENNEDY: Ran a clean and fair campaign in which Chicago Mayor Richard Daley clearly didn't have thousands of dead people voting in order to swing Illinois Kennedy's way.

RONALD REAGAN: Former actor. Rather than running for and winning election, he simply pretended he already was president and moved into the White House, staying for eight years.

DICK CHENEY: Found a likable, regular-guy son of a former president to pose as president and let Cheney pull the levers of power from behind the scenes.

---

[5] That's Swedish for "fresh cheese," meaning "unique and not yet foul-smelling."

Confused? Me too. Wait, not me too. I'm not confused in the slightest. In fact, I've written this book to help you do a "dry run"[6] for your presidential campaign. Trust me, I've thought of everything I can think of. If you work through the scenarios and exercises herein, you will be better prepared for the rigors of an actual election. If Al Gore had been able to read this book before his presidential run[7] he would now have, instead of an Academy Award, the raging acid reflux all presidents get and deserve.

Can I guarantee victory? No. But I can guarantee fun![8] The book is broken down into three main sections:

QUALIFICATIONS AND PARTY AFFILIATION

In this section we will determine if you have the basic stuff to run for president and, following that, whether you're more elephant, donkey,[9] or whatever animal may be associated with an independent candidate.[10]

THE PRIMARIES

In this section you will challenge the contenders of your own party in a series of tests and obstacles that will make the hijinks on *Battle of the Network Stars* look like *Masterpiece Theatre*.

---

[6] A "dry run" is a simulation of an actual event conducted for the purpose of practice. Not to be confused with "dry hump," which is simulated intercourse over the clothes.

[7] And maybe one more sympathetic Supreme Court justice, or a few thousand old people in Florida who could figure out how to vote properly, or the sense to run on Clinton's record rather than away from it . . .

[8] Depending on your definition of fun.

[9] I hope that, in actuality, you're neither an elephant nor a donkey, since non-human species are ineligible for office.

[10] House cat? Swiss person?

THE GENERAL ELECTION

If you survive the primaries, you'll face off against your rival from the other party in the general election. The prize? The presidency (except not really, because we're just pretending here).

Let's hit the road! If you flip to the back of the book,[11] you'll see that I've provided a handy scorecard[12] with which to track your progress toward 1600 Pennsylvania Avenue. During the primaries, you will be attempting to amass enough delegates to win the nomination.[13] In the general election, you're gunning for electoral votes. If you manage to successfully navigate all the challenges, you'll be ready for the sequel to this book, *So You'd Like to Be Re-Elected President?*

So let's get going—that is, if you really still want to be president.

---

[11] Go ahead; I'll wait.

[12] If you did flip to the back, you probably noticed that only one scorecard is provided. Whatever you may be thinking, do not photocopy the scorecard so that multiple people may enjoy working through the challenges. Everyone should buy his own book.

[13] This book has been rigged to dissolve to dust in your hands if you fail to earn the nomination.

★★

In theory, there are only two qualifications to running for president of the United States, so we're going to cover those first. For each question below, check the box that most closely reflects your answer.

1. I am at least 35 years of age.

( ) Yes   ( ) No   ( ) Don't Know

2. I am a natural-born United States citizen.

( ) Yes   ( ) No   ( ) Don't Know

If you answered "Yes" to both questions, nicely played! You've met the minimum requirements to be elected president of the United States. If you answered "No" to one or both of them, don't panic. As I'm about to explain, you're not sunk yet.[1]

If you're not yet thirty-five years old, there's a simple solution, derived from my experience in Mikey Lobedel's basement in the summer of 1987. At that time, I was only seventeen, a full four years short of the legal drinking age. Fortunately, Mikey was a genius artist and stenciler and had created a poster board, life-sized mock-up of an Illinois driver's license. You simply gave Mikey

---

[1] If you answered "Don't know" to either question, please make an appointment with your primary care physician posthaste. Bring this book with you; you know how waiting rooms are.

thirty-five dollars, stood in front of a white screen with your head framed in the driver's-license picture hole, smiled for the birdy, and then waited for Mikey to work the heavy-duty laminator he'd boosted from the YMCA.[2] *Voilà!* A fakey good enough to fool just about every alcoholic liquor-store employee in the tri-county area, no matter how runty, pimply, and obviously pubescent the cardholder was at the time.

The bad news for those of you readers under thirty-five is that I lost touch with Mikey Lobedel many years ago, so you're going to need to track him down on your own.[3] The good news is that the famously incurious press probably won't bother verifying the ID's validity. The other bad news is that if you do find Mikey, regardless of your gender, race, or physical proportions, you're going to have to change your name to Lanny Lipschitz,[4] and you're 5'7", weigh 145 pounds, and were born on 4/31/66.[5]

If you answered "No" to the second question above, things get a bit trickier. Unfortunately, this shit is written into the constitution, which is notoriously difficult to change. If we haven't yet been able to codify equal rights for women or to deny equal rights to homosexuals, altering one of the fundamental underpinnings to electing our chief executive seems like a long shot.

The trick is to become so beloved that a majority of voters in three-quarters of the states will vote for your amendment so that they can then elect you president. (The good news is that if you're able to pull *that* off, winning the election will be a piece of cake.)

---

[2] Which used it for pool passes and children's crafts—and leaves, lost keys, toe jam and anything else the bored teenager behind the desk felt like laminating.

[3] Though my hunch is he's still in his basement working on cultivating what he called "super weed," which (Mikey claimed, anyway) not only got you high, but actually *increased* your IQ.

[4] At any given time there were no fewer than four hundred Lanny Lipschitzes trying to purchase alcohol in the northern suburbs of Chicago.

[5] Yes, I'm aware there are only thirty days in April, but Mikey Lobedel wasn't. Beware the "super weed."

Granted, there aren't many people who could become popular enough to achieve this, and unless I've already heard of you, odds are you have a long way to go in order to reach that level. You need to get busy building a personal profile and list of accomplishments that will compel a couple hundred million Americans to throw aside 230-plus years of history.

At this stage, I think it would be useful to take a look at my in-depth analysis of the current crop of contenders for first foreign-born president of the United States to see who might have a head start on the pack.

See chart on right.

Do you see yourself in any of these people?[6] If so, you may have what it takes to become the first foreign-born president of the United States—though you should get the constitutional amendment process moving, since that takes a while and you'll want to make sure you're able to run before you get too old,

NAME	PLACE OF ORIGIN
GOV. ARNOLD SCHWARZENEGGER	Austria
BONO	Ireland
DR. HENRY KISSINGER	Germany
SPONGEBOB SQUAREPANTS	Bikini Bottom, Pacific Ocean
ALBERT EINSTEIN	Germany

---

[6] If you see yourself in Gisele Bündchen, feel free to contact me via the publisher.

PROS	CONS
• Already holds elective office. • Muscle-bound like a superhero. • Box-office receipts could help bring down budget deficit. • First Lady–ready wife.	• Odd accent plays up fact he really is a foreigner. • Penchant for Speedos. • Compared to rest of U.S., California is a foreign country, making Schwarzenegger twice removed from eligibility.
• Rock star. • Renowned humanitarian. • Has both George W. Bush and Nelson Mandela on speed dial. • Rock star.	• Messiah complex. • Some of the songs start to sound the same after awhile. • The Edge has no interest in vice president job.
• Very experienced.	• War criminal.
• Cross-species appeal: friends with starfish, octopus, and scuba-diving squirrel. • Blue-collar job (fry cook) makes him highly relatable to average voter.	• Lacks experience. • Cartoon character.
• Super smart. • If asked at a press conference, "Who do you think you are—Einstein?", could answer, "Yes." • Hair.	• Pacifist. • Died in 1955.

continued on next page

particularly if you're following the Gisele Bündchen template.

If you don't see yourself in any of my handy models, don't despair too much, since it's unlikely you are going to be elected president anyway.

But don't let that stop you from continuing on your reading journey.

NAME	PLACE OF ORIGIN
GUY WHO DRIVES IN THE WINNING RUN TO LEAD THE CHICAGO CUBS TO THEIR FIRST WORLD SERIES TITLE SINCE 1908	Not yet known, but likely someplace in Latin America
GISELE BÜNDCHEN	Some sort of magical place where the rivers flow with milk
ZIGGY STARDUST	Mars

PROS	CONS
• Instant folk hero. • High name recognition. • Has Illinois electoral votes in the bag.	• May never happen.
• Super hot.	• None that I can think of.
• Elevator boots provide commanding stature. • Strong supporter of space program. • Spiders from Mars make handy choices for cabinet members.	• America probably not ready for androgynous cross-dressing president from outer space.

BUT ARE YOU
REALLY QUALIFIED?

How Much Baggage
Are You Carrying?

While the explicit requirements to run for president are minimal, even a cursory review of those who have previously held the office—or even won the nomination of a major party—reveals certain implicit requirements to win the election.

I've divided these qualifications into two categories: merits and demerits. Simply go through the lists below and check each statement that you feel applies to you.

This is your first chance to earn or lose delegates, so break out the scorecard provided in the back of the book, and keep a tally of your points as you go.

First, the merits. Each of the following is identified with a someone who has either been elected president or won a party's nomination. For each merit you check, give yourself 5 delegates.

No, seriously, go get the scorecard, that's why I had them print that page. It cost extra to do that and it would be a shame if it wasn't used for its specific purpose[1].

---

[1] If you do indeed detach and use the scorecard, please contact me through the publisher's Web site, www.towbooks.com, and say so. I'll be collecting the responses so I can say "I told you so" to the bean counters who tried to crush my creativity.

MERITS

I have:

___ Driven a car into a river and drowned a woman.

___ The childhood nickname "Bubba."

___ Smoked marijuana (but didn't inhale).

___ Had numerous extramarital affairs and plans to continue doing so even if elected president.

___ Like a *billion dollars* in the bank.

___ Had sexual intercourse with and impregnated a slave girl.

___ Provided unwavering military leadership in beating back the Nazi menace.

___ A penchant for stovepipe hats.

___ Trouble not drinking alcohol.

___ Had trouble with excess drinking in the past, but that's truly behind me, no doubt about it.

___ Been a United States senator.

___ Served honorably in the military, even seeing combat.

___ Not only served honorably in the military, but saw combat and was even either wounded or held as a prisoner of war.

___ Had "other priorities" during a time of war.[2]

___ Smoked marijuana (and did inhale, but didn't like it).

___ Served as governor of a populous state.

___ Shot a man during a duel (but not just to watch him die).

___ Starred in a movie opposite a chimpanzee.

___ A very embarrassing sibling.[3]

___ Halitosis.

___ Chopped down a cherry tree.

___ Plagiarized a major speech.

___ Founded a university.

___ Cartoonishly large ears.

---

[2] Like getting three different masters degrees, a law degree, a certificate from the Barbizon School of Beauty, and essentially anything else I could think of to keep from getting my ass shot off.

[3] We're talking something major like he/she has a beer named after him, not just have a funny haircut, or one of those ties that looks like piano keys.

___ Run several failed businesses.

___ Interesting glasses.

___ A close relative who was president.

___ Children who hate me.

___ Married my second cousin.

___ Been president of a Major League Baseball franchise.

Okay, now that the merits are out of the way, let's get to the demerits—things that, at least thus far,[4] have been deal breakers when it comes to getting nominated by a major party. For each demerit you circle, subtract 5 delegates from your total.

DEMERITS

I am:

___ Hispanic

___ Black

___ Female

___ Jewish

Pretty short list, huh? Sure, It eliminates a good 65–70% of the American population, but the primary fields are plenty crowded already with all those white guys. Imagine the confusion if *everyone* had a shot.

Alrighty, the warm-up is over. It's time to get into the heavy exercise portion of our journey.

Hold on to your giblets. It's going to get rocky.

---

[4] It is possible, maybe even probable that by the time this book is published at least one of the entries to follow can be crossed off. If this is the case, please do so with my blessing.

ELEPHANT, DONKEY, OR SOME KIND OF ELEPHONKEY?

Your Place on the Political Spectrum

★★

In America, you can belong to only one team at a time. Yankees fans don't also root for the Red Sox, Cubs fans wish for a fiery-hot death[1] to rain down on followers of the White Sox, and anyone with any sense loathes the Dallas Cowboys. You can't be two opposite things at once—animal *and* vegetable, liquid *and* solid, pop *and* rock. You either swing one way, or the other, unless you're Anne Heche, or *Transformer*-era Lou Reed.

Therefore, before the race begins in earnest, it's time to figure out which team you'll seek to represent in the battle: the Republicans or the Democrats. During the primaries, different positions will produce different responses depending on your team. What plays well with the Christian Coalition may have the ACLU burning you in effigy. It's also important at this stage that you give up any thoughts of running as an independent—that is, unless you'd like to give up the idea of being president, as well.[2]

Personally, I hate labels and stereotypes. I've never understood why it's strange for a heterosexual male to wear out his VHS copy of *Steel Magnolias* or believe that leg warmers are unisex apparel. But we are a nation of segregation, of separation, and the only route to

---

[1] Not literal hot death. ... Okay, I admit it; actual hot death.

[2] If you fancy yourself running as part of the Libertarian, Green, Constitution, Mandy Moore Rox or any other party besides the two major ones, let me recommend *Marginal Political Movements for Dummies* for further reading.

17

electoral victory is to divide and conquer by making sure your half is bigger than the other guy's.[3] You may feel as if you already know which team you belong to, and you may even have shown loyalty via the voting booth in the past. But—as Thomas Frank showed us in his seminal book, *What's the Matter With Kansas?* and its sequel, *Seriously, What the Fuck, Oklahoma?*—some people actually vote against their own best interests out of a misplaced or misinformed sense of loyalty.

You wouldn't want to be the standard-bearer for a party whose platform you didn't actually believe in (unless you're Rudy Giuliani), would you? I didn't think so, which is why your next exercise is to see exactly where you fall on the political spectrum. Are you a right-wing conservative (Attila the Hun)? A far-right-wing conservative (Pat Robertson)? A bicycle-riding, vegan, Berkeley-living, no-nukes leftist (someone with ratty hair, who probably smells)? Or are you somewhere in the middle (pretty much all the rest of America)? Take the following quiz to find out.[4]

Different answers will direct you toward one party or the other. Think of it as a kind of tug-of-war for your political soul—although, considering that all politicians must forfeit their souls as a prerequisite to running for elective office, maybe think of it instead as a tug-of-war for your body, which has to do all the campaigning anyway.

Each answer can earn you points in either the Republican (example: **+1R**) or Democratic (example: **+1D**) columns. Some answers will be party-neutral (indicated as **+0**). Keep a running tally for both parties, and at the end, we'll finish up with some math. Don't worry; it'll be easy.

---

[3] Or by having a sympathetic Supreme Court.

[4] PLEASE NOTE: The scoring for each question will be printed just below the question. I was going to ask the publisher to print the scoring information backwards, requiring you to hold the book up to a mirror, but then I realized that if this book is going to be read at all, it'll likely be while you're sitting on the toilet, and a mirror might not be handy, or at least it will be difficult to reach while you're doing your dirty business. Ergo, the smaller font.

For the first set of questions, indicate your level of agreement or disagreement with each statement.

1. THE GOVERNMENT'S HIGHEST PRIORITY SHOULD BE CONTROLLING THE NATIONAL DEBT.

( ) STRONGLY AGREE ( ) AGREE ( ) DISAGREE ( ) STRONGLY DISAGREE

+0 STRONGLY AGREE +0 AGREE +0 DISAGREE +0 STRONGLY DISAGREE

Agreement with this statement used to be a reliable indicator of conservatism, but the national debt has exploded under President Bush after having been trimmed significantly under President Clinton, so now, who the hell knows?

2. THE GOVERNMENT'S SECOND HIGHEST PRIORITY SHOULD BE GETTING OLD PEOPLE TO SWITCH OFF THEIR BLINKERS WHEN THEY'RE NOT TURNING.

( ) STRONGLY AGREE ( ) AGREE ( ) DISAGREE ( ) STRONGLY DISAGREE

+0 STRONGLY AGREE +0 AGREE +0 DISAGREE +0 STRONGLY DISAGREE

Okay, this doesn't really have anything to do with politics, but I really hope, for all our sakes,[5] that just about everyone answered "Strongly agree." I promise my next question will be relevant. I'm new at this whole political orientation quiz, thing. I'm sure I'll get better.

3. THE GOVERNMENT TAKES TOO MUCH OF MY MONEY, AND NOT ENOUGH OF OTHER PEOPLES'.

( ) STRONGLY AGREE ( ) AGREE ( ) DISAGREE ( ) STRONGLY DISAGREE

+2D STRONGLY AGREE +1D AGREE +1R DISAGREE +2R STRONGLY DISAGREE

Odds are that if you answered "Strongly agree" or "Agree," you feel the impact of taxes, which makes you poor, which probably makes you a Democrat.

4. THOSE WITH MORE MONEY HAVE THE RIGHT TO SUPERIOR MEDICAL CARE, INCLUDING BUYING BLACK-MARKET KIDNEYS FROM HOMELESS PEOPLE.

( ) STRONGLY AGREE ( ) AGREE ( ) DISAGREE ( ) STRONGLY DISAGREE

+2R STRONGLY AGREE +1R AGREE +1D DISAGREE +2D STRONGLY DISAGREE

This question is designed to test the strength of your belief in a free market. A true conservative believes anything and everything should be for sale, including vital organs.

5. PEOPLE SHOULD REFER TO MARIJUANA AS "WACKY TOBACKY."

( ) STRONGLY AGREE ( ) AGREE ( ) DISAGREE ( ) STRONGLY DISAGREE

+3R STRONGLY AGREE +2R AGREE +1D DISAGREE +2D STRONGLY DISAGREE

If you call dope "wacky tobacky" you are either old or hopelessly square and therefore likely to lean Republican. If you think a better name would be "demon weed," add two more points to the Republican column. If you can think of more than ten additional euphemisms for marijuana[5], add seven more points to the Democratic column.

6. I BELIEVE THE GOVERNMENT SHOULD HAVE FREE REIN TO SPY ON ITS CITIZENS BECAUSE ONLY CRIMINALS AND TERRORISTS HAVE SOMETHING TO HIDE.

( ) STRONGLY AGREE ( ) AGREE ( ) DISAGREE ( ) STRONGLY DISAGREE

+4R STRONGLY AGREE +3R AGREE +3D DISAGREE +4D STRONGLY DISAGREE

Disagreeing makes you not only a Democrat, but a target of suspicion as well. Did you use a credit card to purchase this book? Did you buy it in a store that has surveillance cameras? If so, government agents know who you are, and they're coming for you.

---

[5] Including, but not limited to: dope, chronic, kind, kind bud, kindly old man, mary jane, creep, creeper, creepage, blunt, spliff, reef, reefer, cheeba, ganja, grass, Irish mind bomb, herb, joint, dank, buddha, dirt weed, doobage, hooba, lopsang, and barbecued iguana.

7. MY FAVORITE TV PROGRAMS ARE *DANCING WITH THE STARS* AND *THE LAWRENCE WELK SHOW.*

( ) STRONGLY AGREE ( ) AGREE ( ) DISAGREE ( ) STRONGLY DISAGREE

+2R STRONGLY AGREE +1R AGREE +1D DISAGREE +2D STRONGLY DISAGREE

If you agreed, you have weird taste in television. You also lean Republican. If your favorite television show is *The 700 Club,* add 75 points to the Republican column. If your favorite program is "Channel 12," you should know that that's not actually a television program.

8. I BELIEVE IN THE ABSOLUTE RIGHT TO FREE SPEECH, EXCEPT FOR RUSH LIMBAUGH, SEAN HANNITY, AND ANN COULTER, WHO SHOULD SHUT THE FUCK UP.

( ) STRONGLY AGREE ( ) AGREE ( ) DISAGREE ( ) STRONGLY DISAGREE

+4D STRONGLY AGREE +3D AGREE +0 DISAGREE +0 STRONGLY DISAGREE

Agreeing here makes you both a Democrat and, I'm sorry to say, a hypocrite, not that I blame you.

9. I BELIEVE THAT BOTH THE BIBLE AND *GIRLS GONE WILD* ARE GOOD SOURCES FOR THE BASIS OF LIVING A MORAL LIFE.

( ) STRONGLY AGREE ( ) AGREE ( ) DISAGREE ( ) STRONGLY DISAGREE

+2D STRONGLY AGREE +1D AGREE +1R DISAGREE +2R STRONGLY DISAGREE

The only better illustration of the wages of sin than the Old Testament is watching fifteen minutes of *Girls Gone Wild 47: Tampa, Tequila, Titties!*

10. GOLF IS NOT A SPORT, BUT BOWLING IS.

( ) STRONGLY AGREE   ( ) AGREE   ( ) DISAGREE   ( ) STRONGLY DISAGREE

+4D **STRONGLY AGREE** +3D **AGREE**   +3R **DISAGREE**   +4R **STRONGLY DISAGREE**

Republicans belong to country clubs. Democrats wear shirts with their names stitched above the pockets. If you think neither golf nor bowling is a sport, congratulations—you're right.

11. THERE'S ONLY ONE GOD: THE MIGHTY ODIN, WHO RULES FROM HIS THRONE IN ASGARD, HIS SON THOR (AND THOR'S MIGHTY HAMMER) BY HIS SIDE!

( ) STRONGLY AGREE   ( ) AGREE   ( ) DISAGREE   ( ) STRONGLY DISAGREE

+2R **STRONGLY AGREE** +1R **AGREE**   +1D **DISAGREE**   +2D **STRONGLY DISAGREE**

Republicans are the party of religion. Also, you probably have far too much of your net worth tied up in comic books.

12. WITH VERY FEW EXCEPTIONS,[6] WE SHOULD LIMIT IMMIGRATION.

( ) STRONGLY AGREE   ( ) AGREE   ( ) DISAGREE   ( ) STRONGLY DISAGREE

+3R **STRONGLY AGREE** +2R **AGREE**   +2D **DISAGREE**   +3D **STRONGLY DISAGREE**

If you agree or strongly agree with this statement, in the back of the book you'll find a petition to change the inscription on the Statue of Liberty from: "Give me your tired, your poor,/Your huddled masses yearning to breathe free,/The wretched refuse of your teeming shore./Send these, the homeless, tempest-tost to me,/I lift my lamp beside the golden door!" to: "Park's closed. Moose out front should've told you."

---

[6] The exception being Swedish chicks.

13. THE BEST SUPER POWER WOULD BE THE ABILITY TO READ OTHER PEOPLE'S MINDS.

( ) STRONGLY AGREE   ( ) AGREE   ( ) DISAGREE   ( ) STRONGLY DISAGREE

+3R **STRONGLY AGREE** +2R **AGREE**   +2D **DISAGREE**   +3D **STRONGLY DISAGREE**

If you agree, you're wrong. The best super power would be telekinesis.[7]

For the next group of questions, choose the answer that, in your opinion, best completes each sentence.

14. MICHAEL MOORE IS _____.

A. an original and important filmmaker who speaks truth to power and should probably have statuary built in his honor

B. someone whose messages I tend to agree with, but I'm often uncomfortable with his tactics and tendency to stretch the truth

C. a hack who bludgeons the truth to make a couple of bucks

D. going to get a punch in the snot locker if I ever see him in person

E. the guy who fixed my muffler

A. **+5D** Obviously you haven't seen *Canadian Bacon*. B. **+3D** C. **+3R** D. **+5R** Whatever you do, make sure his cameras aren't rolling. E. **+0** Congratulations. You have a healthier relationship with popular culture than I do.

---

[7] Let's just dispense with the B.S. arguments and recognize that if you have the power to move objects with your mind, you could both fly (by moving *yourself* with your mind) and be invisible (by bending light in a certain way around). Don't tell me "That can't be done"! We're talking about super powers, for the love of God! You always pull this crap when we're just trying to engage in a little fun speculation.

15. I THINK _____ IS A REASONABLE RESPONSE TO THE ISSUE OF GLOBAL WARMING.

A. an executive order banning cars and mandating bicycles

B. government regulation that seeks to reduce or restrict the use of fossil fuels and the emission of greenhouse gases while giving industry a reasonable amount of time to comply in order to cause minimal disruption

C. stockpiling canned goods, water, weaponry, and a shitload of porn in an underground bunker

D. that recycling when I think of it and when it's convenient

E. that as long as there are birds in the sky and fish in the sea the enviro-nazis will continue to restrain free trade and progress and that, therefore, buying an eighteen-wheeler for my four-mile commute to work

A. **+7D** B. **+1D** C. **+3R** D. **+0** E. **+25R** Vice President Cheney, is that you?

16. ON A TYPICAL SUNDAY, I _____.

A. listen to NPR's *Weekend Edition* with Liane Hansen, after which I repair hummingbirds' broken wings at the local wildlife shelter. Evenings, I contemplate the suffering of people in the third world as I eat my dinner of tree bark and thatch

B. tackle the latest home improvement project, then take a nap in front of the tube with the game on

C. spend quality time with my spouse and family

D. eat pancakes

E. worship at the denomination of my choice, after which I don my special Sunday hair shirt and engage in the immolation of my flesh as atonement for my sins of the past week

A. **+5D** B. **+0** C. **+3R** If your "quality time" involves some kind of secret dungeon sex play, **+5D**. D. **+0** Me too. E. **+12R**

17. THE MAINSTREAM MEDIA _____.

A. are nothing but lapdogs and stenographers for the Republican administration

B. generally try to be objective, but often betray an institutional bias by gravitating toward the sensational or entertaining angle

C. are full of crap, no matter what they're saying about whom

D. hate President Bush and wishes for his downfall

E. actively root for Al-Qaeda and the Taliban to take over our country

A. +5D B. +1D C. +0 D. +3R E. +7R

18. ABORTION SHOULD BE _____.

A. as convenient as a Starbucks drive-thru

B. ultimately a woman's choice

C. discouraged as much as possible, but legal in cases of rape or incest, or to protect the health of the mother

D. illegal, except to protect the health of the mother

E. illegal, except if my idiot teenager gets knocked up and is going to piss her life away by having the baby and getting married to some dickweed whose chief ambition is to be the number one pump jockey at the Gas 'n' Sip

A. +30D They'll be right next to Prostate Exams 'R' Us (just listen for the guys saying, "Oof!"). B. +5D C.+2D D. +1R E. +5R

19. WAR _____

A. … What is it good for? Absolutely nothing. Say it again—hunh!

B. Pigs is my favorite Black Sabbath song.

C. is rarely, but sometimes, necessary to protect our national interests.

D. is a useful weapon in the American foreign policy arsenal.

E. would end more quickly if we used bigger bombs.

A. **+10D** Let's get together sometime and you can tell me about how you almost died from the brown acid at Woodstock. B. **+2D** C. **+0** D. **+2R** E. **+9R**

20. THE DEATH PENALTY _____.

A. should never be used, not even if Kitty Dukakis were to be raped and murdered

B. is okay in theory but impossible to implement in practice, as too many innocent people wind up on death row

C. should be reserved for the most heinous of crimes

D. takes too long when it comes to the appeals process

E. should be expanded to include such things as jaywalking or putting "My Cairn Terrier Is Smarter Than Your Honor Student" bumper stickers on your car

A. **+9D** B. **+3D** C. **+0** D. **+2R** E. **+7R** If you add "dumping your car ashtray full of cigarette butts at the toll booth" to the list, count me in.

That's the end of the political persuasion quiz! Now, tally your total points in each column and subtract the smaller number from the larger one. The result is your political persuasion score.

The following chart will give you some idea how you compare to other famous political personages.

+100D	+75D	+50D	+25D
• Dirty hippies • The love child of Ted Kennedy and Gloria Steinem	• Rosie O'Donnell • Dan Rather • Stalin	• Jane Fonda • Jimmy Carter	• Richard Nixon[8] • Al Gore

+25R	+50R	+75R	+100R
• Bill Clinton[9] • Dwight Eisenhower	• Ronald Reagan	• Pol Pot • Rush Limbaugh	• Lord Voldemort • Dick Cheney

From this moment forward you are either a Republican or a Democrat. Try not to forget which, or you might do something foolish like determine your position on a particular issue via a weighing of the facts as opposed to a knee-jerk decision predicated on your party affiliation. Such free-thinking could prove fatal to your candidacy.

---

[8] Talked to the commies, reduced the number of nukes, passed landmark environmental legislation.

[9] Cut the deficit, trimmed welfare benefits, came from the South, had a fondness for big-boned gals.

ARE YOU REALLY SURE YOU WANT TO BE PRESIDENT?

Plowing Past the Fail-Safe Point

★★

Any moment now, you're going to turn the page and find that you're actually reading a chapter that is part of the journey towards election, but before we get there, it's time to launch an exploratory committee of your soul and really make sure that you're prepared to embrace the rigors of the presidency.

If you become president, you're looking at fifteen-hour workdays, sleepless nights, and an endless onslaught of crises. But really, that just describes the typical life of anyone with kids under the age of four. No, there's a special toll to being president … a price beyond your time, your energy, or your family life.

That price? Your looks.

Believe it. Being president ruins whatever looks you might have. You may enter the White House as Hotty McHotterson, but you'll exit Baron Von Haggard of Homelytown.[1]

Don't believe me? Let's look at the photographic evidence.

BILL CLINTON

In 1992, William Jefferson Clinton was slim (relatively) and smiling—the veritable picture of youthful horndog vigor.

After eight years of harassment, investigation, near-impeachment, and a cramping of his ability to score quality poontang, we

---

[1] Or Princess Heinous of Hagville, if you prefer.

see a gray-haired guy who'd have a hard time getting a date at the Sunny Heights Nursing Home and Bingo Parlor.

BEFORE   AFTER

GEORGE WASHINGTON

Washington was a relatively young fifty-seven when he entered office. One would think the worry of leading the colonial army in its struggle against the British Empire would have etched some age into his features, but he was surprisingly youthful-looking when he took the oath of office.

After enduring eight years in office and turning down a popular request to essentially name himself president for life, Washington retired to Mt. Vernon looking all of his sixty-five years and then some.

BEFORE   AFTER

GROVER CLEVELAND

Early in his life, our twenty-second and twenty-fourth president was known around his native New Jersey as "The Brushy-'Stached Stud Muffin."

By the end of his final term, the only nickname Cleveland had any business responding to was "Fat-Ass."

BEFORE   AFTER

GEORGE W. BUSH

One of the more regular-guy handsome men to hold the presidency, a fifty-four-year-old Bush took office looking fit, tan, rested, and more than ready for his close-up.

By 2007, an ill-conceived war, low approval ratings, and a couple of booze-hound daughters had taken their toll.

BEFORE   AFTER

JOHN F. KENNEDY

Finally, let's look at our youngest, most dashing President, the one who had the ultra-glamorous wife, and who got his illicit nookie from movie stars instead of chubby interns.

BEFORE   AFTER

Let's just say no one looks good under a tombstone.[1]

If all that hasn't dissuaded you, then turn the page and begin your quest to become the next president of the United States!

---

[1] And no starlet is going to have sex with him unless Paris Hilton is a necrophiliac.

THE PRIMARIES

Declaring that you're seeking the nomination is cool and all, but in terms of a lasting legacy, it doesn't get you very far. Let me drop some names on you, rapid-fire:

MORRIS UDALL   AL BUNDY

ALAN CRANSTON   LAMAR ALEXANDER

PETE DU PONT   PAUL TSONGAS

Which name did you find most recognizable? Al Bundy? Exactly. Al Bundy is, of course, the fictional character played by actor Ed O'Neill in the Fox sitcom *Married With Children,* which stopped airing better than ten years ago and wasn't all that great to begin with. The rest of those names belong to politicians who failed to win their party's nomination during the primary battle.

That's not to say that all primary challengers go down in obscurity. Walter Mondale was routed in the 1976 Democratic primary by Jimmy Carter before getting his shot at the top of the ticket so that he could get routed by Ronald Reagan in the 1984 general election. Ronald Reagan himself lost the 1976 Republican primary, yet went on to have both an airport and a revolution named after him. Other primary losers include Alexander Haig, Pat Robertson, and Donald Rumsfeld.

That said, my hunch is you'd rather secure your legacy by being president rather than by being a guy who tried to seize control of the presidency from a podium, a religious nutcase who thinks hurricanes are God's punishment for homosexuals, or the most disastrous defense secretary this side of Robert McNamara.

So remember that if you're in it, you're in it to win—or at least to do well enough to be chosen as a running mate. That's not a bad gig either.

Let's get to it! The moment has arrived to announce your candidacy to the world. Maybe.

ANNOUNCING YOUR CANDIDACY
Meeting Tim Russert

Your exploratory committee has found the answer they were looking for: Indeed you *should* put yourself forward to be the next president of the United States. It's time to man the megaphone and declare your intentions to the world.

There's lots of different ways to announce that you're running for president: calling a press conference, posting it on your website, releasing a statement to the wire services, hiring a team of skywriters, or drawing your declaration in a field of snow with a stream of your own urine. But there's no better megaphone than *Meet the Press*, hosted by Tim Russert. Not only do something like six million people watch[1] *Meet the Press* each week, but also it's a given that whatever you say on the program will be endlessly sliced, diced, and hashed by every other news program, radio talk-show, blog, and the *Grey's Anatomy* chat room.

If Tim Russert is willing to talk to you, you're immediately an A-list politician, more Lindsay Lohan than Tara Reid. The rub is that Tim Russert is widely considered to be the toughest interviewer around.[2] Tim Russert maintains a staff of sixty to seventy thousand

---

[1] Albeit while wiping sleep out of their eyes, nursing a hangover, or eating pancakes.

[2] This is actually a misconception. The toughest interviewer, bar none, is radio host Howard Stern. Ask yourself: Would you rather be grilled on inconsistencies in your policy positions or be badgered into admitting your favorite sexual position/how often you masturbate/look at porn/do anal?

researchers[3] dedicated to knowing everything there is to be known about each interviewee and to backing it up with video, documents and direct quotes. There's nothing that can be hidden from Tim Russert. Tim Russert knows all. Tim Russert has an uncanny ability to find your absolute weakest spot and drive one of his meaty Irish thumbs into that spot until you are very sore indeed. You cannot lie to Tim Russert. Tim Russert is not to be enjoyed; he is not to be defeated, nor bested. Tim Russert is to be weathered; Tim Russert is to be survived. But if you do survive, the rewards can be great.

Just as with hurricanes, there are different categories—different severities—of Tim Russert.

CATEGORY 1: EXCEEDINGLY MILD TIM RUSSERT.

Reserved for frequent guests of his weekly panel: David Brooks, William Safire, Doris Kearns Goodwin. Periods of semilegitimate questions punctuated by lots of smiling, guffawing, and mutual backslapping.

CATEGORY 2: MODERATE TIM RUSSERT.

Appears when guest is a fellow journalist who has authored a topical book. Occasional Russert gusts in the form of official denials from the subject of the book at hand, but no reason to evacuate.

CATEGORY 3: MODERATELY SEVERE TIM RUSSERT.

Conditions are right for a moderately severe Russert when the guest is a frequent one known for being a "straight shooter," e.g., Newt Gingrich or Joe Biden. Steady, sustained Russert questions, including direct examples of guest's previous hypocrisy. The most devastating effects are often mitigated by return bloviation from guest.

---

[3] Working with a budget in the hundreds of millions.

CATEGORY 4: SEVERE TIM RUSSERT.
Steady, sustained Russert questions with frequent gusty follow-ups pressing for direct answers. Most often seen with politicians who are considering a run for president but refuse to give a straight answer on their intentions, or embattled administration officials.

CATEGORY 5: EXTREMELY SEVERE TIM RUSSERT.
A Category 5 Russert has never been observed, but researchers theorize one would appear if someone were to directly insult Russert's father (Big Russ) or the Buffalo Sabres.

For your appearance, you can expect a Category 3 Russert. A Category 4 or higher is unlikely, because you have wisely chosen to pay the proper homage to *Meet the Press* by announcing your candidacy there.

Still, a Category 3 is nothing to be trifled with, and a misstep or two could turn it into a Category 4 with very little warning. This is why I have created a *Meet the Press* candidacy announcement rehearsal in the form of the next quiz.

Through an exhaustive analysis of hours[4] of tape, I've detected a definite pattern to the Russert candidate interview. We're going to walk through this pattern, question by question. Following each question, I will give you four possible answers. Different numbers of delegates will be awarded for each answer, depending on your previously determined party affiliation. Pick the answer you think will most successfully curry favor with voters from your particular political party.

Because I don't know anything about you, I've used my own life and background for this hypothetical grilling. Just remember that the specifics aren't important. In fact, I urge you to forget the specifics pretty much as quickly as you read them, because they're incredibly embarrassing.

---

[4] Okay, three.

1. THE INTRODUCTION AND WELCOME

The typical *Meet the Press* candidate interview starts with an introduction by Russert in the form of a mini-biography that contains at least one notable achievement but always ends with a subtle dig by Tim mentioning a potentially embarrassing failure. Here's how Tim Russert might introduce and welcome me.

> *This Sunday, our "Meet the Candidates" series continues with John Warner. No, not the senator from Virginia, but some other guy whose highest elected offices were recording secretary at his fraternity and president of the Shakira Fan Club. Sometimes after he urinates, he drips a little into his underwear. John, welcome to* Meet the Press.

A. Thanks, Tim. It's a pleasure to be here.

B. If only I was the other John Warner, eh Tim. I would've banged that piece of ass, Elizabeth Taylor ... huh ... huh.

C. That dribbling thing is a flat out lie, Tim.

D. Baba Booey!

A. Republican or Democrat, **+5 delegates**. Simple, straightforward, with almost no likelihood of angering Russert. B. Republican, **+5**. Democrat, **+3**. Senator John Warner is a longtime Republican senate icon and will pay off with potential GOP voters. Sex is on the mind of liberals most of the time, so implying that you'd like to "bang" Elizabeth Taylor, even in her bloated, post-prime years, will gain you some support. C. Republican, **+0**. Democrat, **+3**. If you come from the "Mommy Party," it's more important to show strength in the face of all charges, though in this case you're risking the wrath of Russert. D. Republican, **–10**. Democrat, **+4**. Invoking an obscure Howard Stern reference will only confuse the typical Republican primary voter, and if they do somehow figure out you're a Howard Stern fan, your candidacy is sunk before it gets out of the harbor. As a Republican, you might as well declare Adolf Hitler, or, worse, Hillary Clinton as your running mate. Democrats, on the other hand, being degenerates themselves, will appreciate the Stern reference.

2. THE OPENING SOFTBALL

Russert almost always starts with at least one easy question that allows the candidate to deliver an open-ended statement. It's his way of putting you at ease and fattening you up for the kill.

Tell America why you want to be president.

A. I'm glad you asked me that, Tim. When I travel this great country of ours, what I see is our great people craving great leadership, and fortunately, "leadership" is my middle name because my parents had the foresight to name me John Leadership Warner.[5]

B. Let me turn that question around, Tim. I'd like to know why America wants *me* to be president, and if they want me to be president, the least they could do to let me know is vote for me or at least send campaign contributions.

C. That's for me to know and for you to find out, Tim.

D. Tim, I've heard there's some cool stuff in the White House ... a bowling alley, a personal chef, a masseuse even. I figure the only I way I'll find out for sure is to become president. If elected, I pledge to let everyone else in on the secret.

A. Republican, **+10**. Democrat, **+0**. Republican voters appreciate politicians who do what they think is best, regardless of the consequences. B. Republican or Democrat, **+5**. I don't know what this means either, but it sounds good, doesn't it? C. Republican, **+0**. Democrat, **+10**. When running as a Democrat. it's important to show strength in the face of meaningless questions. D. Republican, **+3**. Democrat, **+7**. Democrats put a higher premium on transparent government.

[5] Not really. My middle name is actually Steadfast.

3. THE INITIAL PROBE

Following the softball, Tim Russert will ask you about something more controversial, but this question won't yet be the heavy artillery. It almost always will involve some sort of youthful indiscretion that may be embarrassing but is rarely fatal. He's trying to get you off balance before he moves in for the kill.

> *It's our understanding that you used to sleep with a stuffed Snoopy toy up until the age of fourteen and perhaps longer, once even insisting that your parents turn the car around after having arrived at the airport to leave for a family vacation because you realized you'd forgotten to pack "Snoopykins." Do you have a comment on this?*

A. No.

B. Was there a Snoopy doll? Sure. Were there Snoopy curtains and a comforter as well? Maybe. Were there Snoopy footy pajamas where ultimately the feet were cut out so I could wear them long past the point of them fitting? Perhaps. Would my parents ever have turned the car around and given in to one of my hysterical crying fits? Never, Tim. Never.

C. What I think people need to ask themselves is whether they want a president who is capable of demonstrating loyalty and constancy, even if that loyalty comes in the form of a bizarre psychological attachment to a stuffed animal he got for Christmas when he was five years old.

D. I don't know where your sources get your information, Tim, but my memory says I ditched Snoopy by twelve at the latest. The blankie, on the other hand, is a different story.

A. Republican or Democrat, **–10.** Danger! Danger! Warning! Warning! Do not stonewall Tim Russert, because he'll be more than happy to ask the same question again except with different, more confrontational wording. In this case, he would follow up with, "We also understand that on the rare occasion your mother was able to pry the doll from your arms so it could get a much-needed cleaning, you would camp out in front of the clothes washer sucking your thumb and whimpering. Still no comment?" **B.** Republican, **+10**. Democrat, **+0**. This answer demonstrates a strong respect for family values, the most important of which is ignoring your kids when they're being bratty. **C.** Republican, **+5**. Democrat, **+5**. Blind loyalty actually plays to primary voters in both parties. **D.** Republican, **+0**. Democrat, **+10**. Democrats seem to gravitate toward flawed, bad-boy types (Kennedy, Clinton) … and going on television and virtually declaring to the nation that your blankie is in the green room is being a bad little boy indeed.

4. STRIKING DEEPER

If you've ever had a root canal, you've experienced this sensation. The dentist begins the drilling, and for the first minute or so you think, "This isn't so bad," but moments later he strikes the nerve and you're begging for the nitrous.[6] This is where Tim Russert is going to display a direct quote, maybe even video, of your own, horrible words.

> *During European History class your junior year of high school, just prior to getting your driver's license, you were quoted as saying, "The only people who get into car accidents are girls and psychos." Is that a position you still hold today?*

A. As you know, Tim, as we get older and wiser our positions evolve. In addition to girls and psychos, I'd now add Asians and old people.

B. Tim, like everyone, there's some things in my past that I regret, and that statement is one of them. The mullet hairdo I rocked during the same era is another. A third is getting wasted at an end-of-the-year party and declaring

---

[6] Or death, either one.

my raging love for Jennifer Schenkenberg in the form of vomiting on her shoes. Would you like me to go on?

C. Let me be clear where I stand on this issue, Tim, and where I stand is with Americans—be they girl, psycho, or anything else under the glorious rainbow that is our country.

D. Fa Fa Flo Hi!

A. Republican, +20. Democrat, −10. Tough on broads, mental illness, and immigrants, all in one fell swoop. The Republican Right just erected a statue in your honor. B. Republican, +10. Democrat, +0. Mullets are very Republican. C. Republican, −10. Democrat, +20. Both sides would correctly read your reference to the "glorious rainbow" as a coded message to the gay community. D. Republican, +0. Democrat, +0. Your third Howard Stern reference in the last fifteen hundred words has little impact on your political fortunes, but it might be enough to get you a mention on his radio show.

5. THE EYE OF THE STORM

Midway through the interview, Russert will throw an inexplicably easy question at you, one that almost can't be botched but is nevertheless dangerous because you've been bracing for the hard stuff. It's like getting a changeup after nothing but hundred-mile-per-hour hard cheese on the inside of the plate. Just answer this one as honestly as you can.

What is your favorite color?

A. Blue.

B. Red, white, and blue, which, coincidentally, are what I bleed, Tim.

C. Chartreuse.

D. Grape.

A. Republican, **+0**. Democrat, **+10**. Blue is associated with peace, which Democrats like. B. Republican, **+10**. Democrat, **+0**. You're a true patriot. C. Republican, **−5**. Democrat, **+5**. I don't know what color this is, but it sounds vaguely French, which is a positive for the traitor wing of the Democratic Party. D. Republican, **−5**. Democrat, **−5**. The headline in the *New York Times* the next day: "Warner Declares Candidacy, Not Sure What a Color Is."

6. THE END OF THE RESPITE

After that brief breather, Russert will be back at it with a question that will be truly embarrassing but likely one you would have expected with proper preparation.

You have Tears for Fears and Phil Collins on your iTunes. We're talking Against-All-Odds Phil Collins, not Genesis-during-their-progrock-years Phil Collins. What America wants to know is: Are you a pussy?

A. You may be right about that music being on my iTunes, Tim, but honestly, who doesn't have some odd music on their iTunes? If I looked at your iTunes, I might find *Judy Garland's Greatest Hits*. I can't recall ever listening to any Phil Collins, and certainly under no circumstances did I sing along with him at full volume in the car with tears streaming down my face.

B. That music is my wife's. I listen exclusively to death metal and jazz.

C. A "pussy" is a cat, Tim. I'm a Homo sapiens.

D. Both underrated artists, Tim. I stand by both "Shout" *and* "Sussudio."

A. Republican, **+0**. Democrat, **+0**. A reasonable denial if I ever saw one, but not one that will curry favor either way. B. Republican, **+10**. Democrat, **−5**. Democrats disproportionately rely on women to win elections, and alienating women rather than just admitting your love for Lite FM is unwise. C. Republican, **−5**. Democrat, **+10**. Another coded message to the gay lobby. D. Republican, **+10**. Democrat, **+5**. If you're a Republican, add 10 delegates if you plan on using Tears for Fears' "Everybody Wants to Rule the World" as your campaign song.

7. THE NINJA DEATH BLOW

The key to any successful ninja death blow is that the victim doesn't see it coming, and so it goes with Tim Russert's penultimate and toughest question during your interview. It will be a question you can't possibly prepare for, no matter how diligent your staff is at unearthing your dirtiest laundry. You just do your best and hope your entire campaign isn't sunk by the mere posing of the question, let alone your answer.

> *In our preparation for this interview, we've come to understand that your marriage proposal to your wife consisted of taking the ring out of your pocket and simply saying, "Here." Is this the act of someone with even a basic amount of human decency, let alone someone who wishes to be president of the United States?*

A. Tim, I've apologized for this unforgivable transgression many times in the form of earrings and other jewelry, and I'm pleased to say that after many years of marriage, my wife has forgiven me.[8]

B. How did you find that out? Did she tell you that?

C. *[Unintelligible, choked sobs of shame.]*

D. The words were only part of that moment in my life, Tim. What people can't know and will never see is the look on my face,[9] which was worth thousands of words.

I'd rather not talk about this one anymore, if that's okay with you. Just give yourself as many delegates as you want. Really. I'm sorry.

---

[8] Sort of, but not really, not that I blame her.

[9] Panic that this smart, beautiful, funny, perfect person for me might say no despite having actually having lived together for six months, having already picked a date, and designed the ring together. Look, I never said *I* was president caliber, okay?

8. THE FRIENDLY FINISHER

One of the great appeals of Tim Russert is his image as a regular guy, despite the fact that he makes millions of dollars and the most powerful people in government fear his phone call. In order to showcase his regular-guy image, Russert will always finish with an innocuous question that allows you to show your regular-person self in return. Once again, honesty is the best policy here. Voters can smell a phony from miles away. For example, they'd never mistake a privileged Yalie who's spent his whole life propped up by his powerful family for a self-made Texas businessman.

And our last question. How about the Bears' chances this year? Super Bowl–bound?

A. From your lips to the football gods' ears, Tim.

B. I hope so, Tim, since I just put sixty G's on them with my bookie.

C. Tim, I'm not worried about frivolous things such as football as long as there's a single person in this country who is suffering or even a little bit blue.

D. As long as they play hard, I'll be proud of them, Tim.

A. Republican, **+10**. Democrats **+0**. Invoking the name of God—even a mythical one that would for some reason care about football—will appeal to Republicans. B. Republican, **–5**. Democrats, **+10**. Likely to play well with the labor-union leadership, if you get what I'm saying.[5] C. Republican, **–10**. Democrats, **–5**. What kind of asshole doesn't care about football? D. Republican, **–20**. Democrats, **+10**. Republicans are winners, not try-harders.

---

[10] What I'm saying is: The popular perception is that illicit gambling, like the labor-union leadership, is often connected to organized crime, like on *The Sopranos*.

Tally your total score. How did you do? If you ended up with a positive number, you have successfully navigated through Tim Russert, and you're now ready to interact with voters.

MONEY-MONEY-MONEY-MONEY ... MONEY!

You and Your Campaign Coffers

★★★

Now that your campaign is up and running, you're in dire need of two things: money and votes, not necessarily in that order. Wait, exactly in that order. Money is the grease that makes the political deep-fryer sizzle.[1] Since there's a good twelve months of campaigning before the first primary vote is even cast, the only way the media can track who is ahead is by (1) making shit up for the sake of stirring controversy, and (2) reporting how much money each candidate has raised.

Without money, you cannot get your message to the people, which means you will not get any votes. It's like the old saying, "Which came first, the chicken or the egg?" In this case, money is both the chicken and the egg, and it's the stuff the chicken eats in order to live, and the nest the chicken lives in, and where the egg incubates, and the antibiotics you pump into the chicken to make sure it doesn't get any disease that makes people froth at the mouth, and the styrofoam container that holds the eggs, and the refrigerated truck that transports the eggs to the store, and the pimply-faced teenager who stocks the eggs in the refrigerator case,

---

[1] If you're a multibillionaire who is willing to risk his or her own capital to run for president, you may skip this chapter and fly in your solid gold private plane directly to your shrink so you can figure out why someone who is a multibillionaire would possibly want to ruin their life by becoming president of the United States.

and the gorilla masquerading as a bagger who manages to crack at least half of every dozen.

Point being, money is everything in politics. It is the alpha *and* the omega, the Peaches *and* the Herb. In fact, we'll probably just elect a big pile of money president before we ever get around to women and Jews and dark people.

YOUR MONEY IQ

To win the election, you're going to need to be as well versed with money as the average Vegas pit boss, or at least a graduate of a top-ten accounting program. So the first round of this quiz is designed just to test your overall money savvy. Each question you answer correctly is worth five delegates.

1. HOW MANY NICKELS ARE THERE IN $1,257,455?

A. A lot!

B. 25,149,100.

C. 2,514,910.

D. I ran out of toes.

E. B or **C**; I'm not sure.

2. IF $50,000 IN PRINCIPAL IS INVESTED WITH AN AVERAGE ANNUAL RETURN OF 10%, HOW MUCH WILL THAT $50,000 HAVE GROWN TO IN FORTY YEARS?

A. Approximately $300,000.

B. A shitload.

C. Approximately $2.1 million.

D. About what the seventh NBA draft pick will receive for his first year in the league.

E. C plus D.

3. STOCK MARKET EXPERT JAMES CRAMER HOSTS A TELEVISION SHOW ON CNBC TITLED:

A. *Crazy Dough*

B. *Mad Money*

C. *Lock This Guy Up Because He's Crazy for the Green Stuff*

D. *Buzzers and Bells, Oh My!*

E. *James Cramer's Money Talk ... Beyotch!*

4. THE PERSON PICTURED ON THE HUNDRED-DOLLAR BILL IS:

A. President Abraham Lincoln.

B. President Benjamin Franklin.

C. President Andrew Jackson.

D. President Thomas C-Note.

E. None of the above.

5. CHOOSE THE APPROPRIATE LYRIC TO FOLLOW THIS LINE FROM THE KANYE WEST SONG "GOLD DIGGER": "NOW I AIN'T SAYIN SHE A GOLD DIGGER ... "

A. ... but she thinks investing in a money market fund is too conservative.

B. ... but she negotiated a much higher salary than the initial offer.

C. ... but she ain't messin with no broke niggas.

D. ... because she'd love me no matter what.

E. ... What I am saying is that she's chilly in the sack.

6. WHEN PLAYING THE BOARD GAME MONOPOLY, WHICH OF THE FOLLOWING IS THE BEST STRATEGY?

A. Concentrate on acquiring the railroads as a steady source of income, then add a quick monopoly in the oranges, reds, or yellows in order to keep your opponents from being able to amass enough money to build on their properties.

B. Baltic, Mediterranean, and Water Works. 'Nuff said.

C. Trade away everything for Boardwalk and Park Place no matter what it costs, and then when no one ever seems to land on it turn after turn after turn, hurl the boardgame pieces/money across the room and storm out in a fit, swearing that they're all cheaters and you're going to hate them forever.

D. Make sure you get the dog playing piece. It has the best luck.

E. Volunteer to be banker. When others pass Go, they get $200. When you pass Go, you get $600.

7. WHICH OF THE FOLLOWING IS THE BEST CREDIT CARD OFFER?

A. Zero annual fee, 15.4% APR. Airline miles earned with each purchase.

B. $50 annual fee, 9.6% APR. Cash back, up to 0.5% of your annual spending.

C. $100 annual fee. Required to pay the balance every month.

D. Free two-liter of Pepsi, a pair of $2 sunglasses, and a coupon for half off at Subway when you sign up for the card.

E. None of the above.

8. WHICH OF THE FOLLOWING REPRESENTS THE BEST INVESTMENT PORTFOLIO?

A. A mix of stocks and bonds, both large and small cap, augmented with CDs and a money market savings account.

B. A strong concentration in emerging foreign markets and new technology.

C. Putting cash in coffee cans and burying them in your yard as you prepare for the inevitable reckoning.

D. Gold.

E. Beanie Babies.

9. TAX DAY IS …

A. April 15th.

B. April 15th, unless it falls on a weekend, in which case the deadline is moved to the next business day.

C. Taxes?

D. The day my hand shakes as I write the check to the IRS.

E. None of the above.

10. WHICH OF THE FOLLOWING ACTIONS IS APPROPRIATE AT A DRIVE-THRU ATM WHEN I AM BEHIND YOU IN LINE?

A. Withdrawing $40 of Fast Cash.

B. Depositing your paycheck and withdrawing a portion in cash.

C. Withdrawing cash for yourself, then for each of your thirty-seven friends inside the car, using a different card each time.

D. Changing deutschmarks into drachmas via the international currency exchange.

E. None of the above.

Give yourself five delegates for each correct answer. **1.** B; **2.** E; **3.** B; **4.** E; **5.** C; **6.** E. **7.** E; **8.** D; **9.** B; **10.** E

Now it gets a bit harder. It's not enough to know all about money; you also have to be able to acquire it in large amounts if you are to have any hope of becoming president. Everyone has different ways of raising scratch when they're desperate for a late-night burrito or a TV ad buy at market saturation levels. With the next quiz, we're going to find out whether you have a roaring pipeline or a meager trickle of cash coming in to your campaign war chest.

Using the following table, identify all the possible avenues you have for acquiring money. Next to each statement is the number of delegates it will earn you.

Searching in the couch cushions for loose change	**(+1)**
Waiting for birthday check from Grandma	**(+3)**
Panhandling outside the train station	**(+3)**
Having your powerful Hollywood friends arrange an intimate gathering for a hundred people for whom cutting $2,300 checks is as easy a decision as green-lighting the next Spider-Man movie	**(+100)**
Holding down a job	**(+3)**
Lottery scratch tickets	**(−3)**
Selling plasma	**(+2)**
Selling sperm	**(+16)**

Selling Ivy League-quality ova to barren Yuppies	(+20)
Selling the energy lobby the right to draft environmental legislation	(+300)
Selling your landscape paintings at local art fairs	(+1)
Inventing something cool and useful, such as a software company that engages in monopolistic practices in order to dominate the market despite its inferior product	(+100)
Grooming your child for a life in showbiz, then stealing her earnings	(+50)
Becoming email buddies with a former Nigerian dictator who has a fortune in bearer bonds stashed away in his home country and just needs a little seed money to liberate it	(+5)
Stealing pennies from the "take a penny, leave a penny" dish at the local convenience store	(+1)
Delivering a speech to a crowd of strangers that is so inspiring, they not only want to vote for you, they wish to shower you in money as well	(+50)
Blow jobs	(+20)
Selling your CD collection	(+1)
Arranging blow jobs for lobbyists	(+80)
Selling your collection of Russian nesting dolls	(+3)
Garage sale	(+5)
Credit cards	(+10)
Buying up Internet domain names like hotmonkeysex.com and licklicklick.com and selling them to porn providers at a premium	(+20)

Hitting mom and dad up for $20—you know, for gas and polling and stuff	(+3)
Pickpocketing	(+5)
Jewel theft	(+20)
Managing a hedge fund	(+50)
Being a former CEO who led a major corporation during a period of lax government oversight and managed to get out prior to indictment	(+75)
Amassing a formidable campaign war chest as senator from New York	(+300)
Being friends with Pauly Shore	(+1)

Go ahead and tally your total delegates earned through this exercise. Hopefully you have at least 500. Any fewer, and you'll be forced to accept public money from the Presidential Election Campaign Fund, which was established to ensure that anyone in the country can afford to lose a presidential election.

FRIEND OR FOE?

You and Your Special Interest Groups

★★

Special interest groups. No, I'm not talking about people who write *Buffy the Vampire Slayer* fan fiction or hang out in the alt.womencrushingbugsunderhighheelswhilewearingsuperherocostumes.com chat room. I'm talking about politically engaged groups organized around single issues. Some are high-profile and deal with broad issues that affect many Americans, e.g., Planned Parenthood and abortion rights, while others have a narrower focus, such as People for the Issuance of a Commemorative Stamp Honoring "Fredo" Corleone, who support ... well, you probably get the idea.

It's important that you be able to quickly identify groups likely to be friendly to you and your candidacy while repelling those that align themselves with the other team. In some cases (example: the "Bring Back *Who's the Boss?*" fan club), a special interest group should be avoided by members of both parties.

It would be far too easy for you to identify a group's ideological alignment if I gave you its actual name. Instead, for this quiz, I've turned each group name into an anagram. First unscramble each anagram, then decide whether the group might be a help to Republicans, Democrats, either, or neither.

In some cases, the anagram may be a clue to the group's identity. In others, it just made me laugh.

UNSCRAMBLE THE ANAGRAM & IDENTIFY PARTY AFFILIATION

1. **AN ANTI-SOCIAL, RAINIEST FOOL**
2. **A NARROWEST OF FEVERINGS**
3. **WINO IN CLAUSTROPHOBIA**
4. **LANK KU-KLUX**
5. **FLOPPIER ETHICAL ATHLETE NOT MERIT MALFEASANT**
6. **HISTORICAL INACTION**
7. **AN INSANITY! O, LET ME RANT**
8. **CRETIN'S DAMN-FOOL ORANGUTAN**
9. **ALIENATE FATIGUED MOAN**
10. **LOONIEST DIRT**

Give yourself 5 delegates for each correct unscrambling and an additional 3 delegates for each correct identification. 1. National Rifle Association. Republican. 2. Veterans of Foreign Wars. Either. 3. Rainbow/PUSH Organization. Democrat.[1] 4. Ku Klux Klan. Neither.[2] 5. People for the Ethical Treatment of Animals. Neither.[3] 6. Christian Coalition. Republican. 7. Amnesty International. Democrat. 8. Lance Armstrong Foundation. Either.[4] 9. Anti-Defamation League. Democrat. 10. Detroit Lions. Neither.[5]

Total your score.

Remember, in politics, you keep your friends close, your enemies closer, and you'll call your mother later, because you're busy running for president.

---

[1] I suppose—though, honestly, with friends like Jesse Jackson, who needs people who might sneak up behind you and stick a knife in your ribs?

[2] Not only are they racist assholes, they're, like, *impossible* to anagram.

[3] That no one actively seeks their endorsement is actually sort of inexplicable considering they have Pamela Anderson-Lee-Rock-Lee-Anderson-Insert the Name of Whoever She's Married to Now Here as spokeswhore. But there you go.

[4] Little-known fact: Originally, the Lance Armstrong Foundation was going to be named the Don't Be a Jerk-Off, Just Wear the Yellow Bracelet Like Everyone Else Foundation.

[5] With a 24 and 72 record between 2000 and 2007, these guys define bad mojo. Your first move as a candidate should be to take out a restraining order on the entire roster.

SHAMELESS PANDERING IS NOT A FACTOR FOR YOU

Appealing to the Primary Voter

★★

As any political pundit will tell you, the primary election is about catering to "the base." But what is "the base?" Let's check Dictionary.com:

1. the bottom support of anything; that on which a thing stands or rests: *a metal base for the table.*

2. a fundamental principle or groundwork; foundation; basis: *the base of needed reforms.*

3. the bottom layer or coating, as of makeup or paint.

4. the principal element or ingredient of anything, considered as its fundamental part: *face cream with a lanolin base; paint with a lead base.*

5. that from which a commencement, as of action or reckoning, is made; a starting point or point of departure.

6. *Baseball.*

    a. any of the four corners of the diamond, esp. first, second, or third base. Compare HOME PLATE.

7. *Military.*

    a. a fortified or more or less protected area or place from which the operations of an army or an air force proceed.

    b. a supply installation for a large military force.

Definition 4 is one I am most interested in, mostly because I've got a small patch of dry skin on the side of my nose and that lanolin stuff sounds like it might do the trick. But it's definition 1 that the political pundits are talking about. In a general election, your political base is the bedrock of your support. They will not desert you, no matter how badly you treat them. They are like Cubs fans, or people who still watch *Lost*: you can abuse their love and trust in the form of heartbreaking losses or impossible-to-follow, never-ending plot threads, and they still remain as loyal as a golden retriever.

Here's a short skit to illustrate the devotion of the political base to their chosen candidate for the *general* election.

CHARACTERS
CANDIDATE
POLITICAL BASE

SCENE 1

(**CANDIDATE** *and* **POLITICAL BASE** *talk to each other on the phone.*)

CANDIDATE   No, I'll totally be there. I wouldn't miss it for the world. Can't wait to be there, as a matter of fact.

POLITICAL BASE   Great. I love you. Do you need money? Up to $2,300[1] is all yours.

CANDIDATE   Sounds perfect. Just make out a check to the campaign.

(**CANDIDATE** hangs up phone.)

POLITICAL BASE   Will do. Hey, while I have you, I was hoping we could talk about ... Hello? ... Hello?

---

[1] This is the limit on individual campaign contributions. If they could, the political base would give much more.

SCENE 2

Interior restaurant, later the same day. **POLITICAL BASE** *sits at a table, absently chewing on a breadstick. An open bottle of wine is mostly drained. Every time the door to the restaurant opens,* **POLITICAL BASE** *sits up like a bird dog waiting for the "retrieve" command.*

POLITICAL BASE   *(To itself)* I sure am worried. I hope nothing bad has happened.

SCENE 3

(Interior same restaurant, later that night. The waiters are busy cleaning up and placing chairs up on the tables.)

POLITICAL BASE   *(To itself)* Man, I'm really starting to get concerned. I'll just go wait outside so he isn't alone if he shows up.

SCENE 4

(Outside the restaurant, hours after the restaurant has closed. **POLITICAL BASE** *sleeps in the dirty gutter, its coat pulled up around its throat.)*

POLITICAL BASE   So cold ... So, so cold ...

SCENE 5

Many weeks later, outside the same restaurant. **POLITICAL BASE** *has been living outside the restaurant since the initial missed meeting, wresting scraps of leftovers from rats in the alley and cleansing itself via tongue baths from stray cats.*

POLITICAL BASE*'s phone rings.*

POLITICAL BASE   Hello?

CANDIDATE   Hey, it's me. Sorry I couldn't make it. Have you been waiting long? Trust me that it couldn't be helped. I'd rather be hanging out with you any day rather than playing footsie with the moderates, but what're you gonna do? You wouldn't believe this, but sometimes they see both sides of an issue and don't wish our opponent would roast in the fiery pits of Hell. I know—crazy, right? Anyway, I need some help. Can you do that? I'm looking for people to go door to door in neighborhoods with my get-out-the-vote message. Now, there's going to be a lot of doors slammed in your face and loogies hocked on your shoes, not to mention the dog attacks, but it's really important, because, believe it or not, some people can't figure out how to register to vote.

POLITICAL BASE *sits up straight, eyes glowing with love and devotion.*

POLITICAL BASE Anything to help. Anything. I'm going to sing "The Wind Beneath My Wings" to you now, if that's okay.

CANDIDATE Whatever, babe.

(CANDIDATE *hangs up phone.)*

As you can see, the devotion of the political base during the general election is nothing short of slavish.[2] However, as the previous illustration also shows, the bases for both parties are—to use a clinical term—batshit crazy. For all their mindless devotion in the general election, during the primaries, if they're in love with one of your competitors or if they feel you've given them the barest slight, they'd just as soon see you slathered in honey and buried in a hill

---

[2] Actually, it's better than slavish since, as far as I know, slaves weren't exactly acting on a volunteer basis.

of fire ants as vote for you. During the primaries, the smallest thing can turn the base against you permanently and irrevocably.

This is why all the experts say it is important to "court" the base. Now, usually when we think of "courting" we picture gentlemen and ladies in the parlor, drinking mint juleps and commenting on the unseasonably hot weather as the prospective couple steal furtive, hopefully meaningful glances at each other and the gentleman prays that at the end of the night he may have the chance to brush his hand against the lady's corset[3] as he moves in to kiss her goodnight on the cheek. It is a ritual of both subtlety and ceremony.

Courting the political base isn't like that. It is not subtle, and it can't be done through coded looks. Courting the political base involves pandering to their interests, no matter how narrow or insignificant. It involves a sacrificing of your principles[4] in the name of currying favor. You will need to do things that, prior to running for president, you never would have imagined doing.

In this way, courting the base is very similar to the once-popular television show *Fear Factor*. For those of you not familiar with the show, each week, six wannabe actors/models (three men, three women) who look disgustingly good in spandex would compete in a series of challenges to see who could best overcome their "fear. "[5] Contestants were eliminated at each challenge until one person was left standing, at which point host Joe Rogan (while silently calculating in his head how much the show was going to earn in syndication) would say, "Congratulations; fear is not a factor for you." A typical sequence of *Fear Factor* events might have been something like this:

1. Contestants are shackled to the steering wheel of a car suspended 600 feet above the Snake River Canyon. They must free themselves from the shackles, break out the car's win-

---

[3] Second base, outside the clothes.

[4] That was a trick. If you have principles, you shouldn't be running for president.

[5] Heights, snakes, cellulite—that kind of thing.

dow and then climb a 40-foot length of razor wire to a safety platform before a flamethrower eats entirely through the cable holding up the car.

2. Contestants are blindfolded and flown in the back of a cargo plane until they are parachuted into the deadly alleys of Caracas, Venezuela. Any contestant who either doesn't lose both of their thumbs to street thugs, or keeps from getting addicted to blow advances to the next round.

3. Contestants run a 100-yard dash while being chased by a cheetah.

4. Contestants eat worms, scorpions, bull testicles and shit like that and wash them down with the blood of virgins.

5. Contestants must stalk and kill a homeless person by driving their thumbs through the homeless person's eye sockets while screaming, "Die, motherfucker, die!"

Fear Factor contestants used to do things like that for a measly $50,000, so you can only imagine what awaits you during the primary season as you compete for a shot at becoming president of the United States.

Just like *Fear Factor,* our next challenge is designed to see how badly you want to win. You must be willing to shamelessly debase yourself in order to earn the loyalty of the political base for your party. This debasement can take many different forms. One is simply having to do something that is silly, pointless, or personally painful, such as driving around in a tank or playing saxophone on *The Arsenio Hall Show.* Another is pledging to enact some kind of obviously idiotic policy once you get into office.

In every case, whatever you do, a little bit of your soul dies in the process, which is actually kind of handy since having a soul makes the work of being president a bit tougher.

Because the debasement will take vastly different forms depending on which party you're trying to represent, this quiz has separate sections for Democrats and Republicans. Simply skip the section that doesn't apply to you.

DEMOCRATS

POVERTY AND HOMELESSNESS

A. Appear at a photo op underneath a bridge, where you're seen putting your arm around a smelly homeless person

B. Appear at a photo op underneath a bridge where you're seen putting your arm around one of your staff members who is dressed up as a smelly homeless person

C. Spend an hour working the line at a soup kitchen, wearing a hairnet

D. Eat "government cheese"[6]

E. Replace your entire campaign staff with homeless people

A. +3 delegates; B. –1; C. +5; D. +7; E. +5

DEATH PENALTY

A. Commission a blue-ribbon panel to investigate the efficacy of the death penalty as a deterrent to crime

B. Propose legislation to replace lethal injection with death by tickling

C. At an impending execution, strap yourself to the electric chair in the place of the condemned inmate while screaming at the prison warden, "Do it! Throw the switch! I dare you! Pussy!"

D. Participate in a series of candlelight vigils outside prisons during executions

---

[6] This may earn you a significant number of delegates, but it will also cause a near-crippling constipation that has the potential to derail your entire candidacy.

E. Commission a blue-ribbon panel to investigate the efficacy of candlelight vigils

A. +5; B. +6; C. +60; D. +1; E. +4

ENVIRONMENT AND GLOBAL WARMING

A. Travel from campaign stop to campaign stop via horse and buggy and/or rickshaw

B. Propose the H_2O Reclaimation Act, requiring everyone to capture and then drink their own bath water

C. Mandate *An Inconvenient Truth* be shown in preschools across America

D. Mandate that Al Gore speak in person in every preschool in America

D. Free sunscreen and tote bag for all campaign donors at the $75 level or above

A. +4; B. −4; C. +2; D. +4; E. +10

ABORTION

A. Get "Roe v. Wade 4eva" tattooed across your back

B. Pledge to appoint Supreme Court justices who will uphold Roe v. Wade or risk a very bad noogie

C. Propose a law making abortion legal up to age 3

D. Wear a pink ribbon or some shit like that around

E. Propose making abortion legal during the first, second, and third trimesters and again when the child is between thirteen and seventeen years of age.

A. +4; B. +2; C. +7; D. +0; E. +25

GUN CONTROL

A. Promise to use Wite-Out on the Second Amendment

B. Promote the use of boomerangs for sport hunting

C. Initiate a "Guns for Buns" program in which people can trade in a gun in exchange for one grope of your buttocks

D. Pledge to "blow away" anyone who opposes you spearheading a ban on assault rifles

E. Promise to "tax the shit out of" the National Rifle Association

A. +3; B. +1; C. +55; D. +0; E. +12

REPUBLICANS

WAR ON TERROR

A. Volunteer to serve a tour of duty in a Middle East hotspot

B. Change the name from "Global War on Terror" (GWOT) to "Global War Where We Ass-Stomp Any Motherfuckers That Get in Our Way" (GWWWA-SAMFERSTGIOW)

C. Change "enhanced interrogation techniques" euphemism for torture to "party time," as in, "We brought a new batch of detainees to Guantanamo, hooked the jumper cables to their genitals, and started party time."

D. Seven words: The Islamic Radioactive Parking Lot of Iran

E. Four more words: Walt Disney Presents Northkorealand

A. +3; B. +5; C. +7; D. +12; E. +10

ABORTION

A. Pledge to make even considering having an abortion a crime

B. Back up "abstinence only" policy by leading by example for the duration of your administration

C. Promise to adopt any unwanted child and keep him in the White House free of charge

D. Increase federal subsidies for adoption

E. Promote new high school sex-ed curriculum, "If You Want Your Cock to Fall Off, Go Ahead and Have Pre-marital Sex, Otherwise, Hands Off the Goodies"

A. +5; B. +100; C. +20; D. −20; E. +10

ILLEGAL IMMIGRATION

A. Pledge to propose a law making it illegal to hire anyone who "talks funny"

B. Commission the U.S. Army Corps of Engineers to build a giant moat around the entire country that would be stocked with piranha … giant piranha

C. To incentivize undocumented Mexican workers to return to their home country, order Taco Bell to create a "Run for the Border and Go Back Across" promotion

D. Require all foreign visitors to get hands stamped at the border in that super-permanent ink some night clubs use that's impossible to wash off and is really embarrassing at work the next day when you're dragging ass and nobody even bothers to ask what's wrong because they know what's wrong is that you didn't actually go to sleep last night and are now trying to power your way through your shitty desk job

E. Make Lou Dobbs Secretary of the Interior

A. +2; B. +4; C. +1; D. +6; E. +8

TAXES AND THE ECONOMY

A. Turn your back to the audience, drop your pants, and, while gripping your butt cheeks, declare, "Read my sphincter—no new taxes."

B. Every time you pledge to give taxpayers "relief," you wink, implying that by "relief" you mean free hand jobs

C. Pledge to rename April 15th "The Government Sodomizes Your Bank Account Day"

D. Campaign slogan: "A chicken in every pot and one of those payday loan places on every corner"

E. Pledge to create "National Half Off Everything" month

A. +4; B. +3; C. +1; D. +1 E. +12

FAITH AND RELIGION

A. Go to church every week

B. Go to church every week and actually sing along with the hymns instead of doing the usual half-assed mumble

C. Propose replacement of execution by lethal injection with crucifixion in order to inject religion back into the public sphere

D. Promise to consider apostles for cabinet positions

E. Give campaign speech at Bob Jones University, titled "God Thinks Black People and White People Kissing Each Other Is Yucky So He Doesn't Want You to Do That"

A. +3; B. +5; C. +12; D. +8; E. +20

Add up your delegates. I hope we've found out that you have what it takes (very few personal convictions, high tolerance for embarrassment, selective amnesia) in order to appeal to your party's base ... because if you don't, your campaign is going to be shorter than the line for a Michael Moore movie in Crawford, Texas.

SHAKING BABIES AND KISSING HANDS, OR IS IT THE OTHER WAY AROUND?

The Primary States

With candidates throwing their hats in the ring before the Inaugural Ball fondue cools from the previous election, the primary campaign season has gotten more bloated than John Belushi's corpse. For sure it's ridiculous, not only because of the time and expense involved, but also because none of it makes any difference.

Traditionally, all the primary marbles have gone into two tiny baskets: the Iowa caucus and the New Hampshire primary. In the past, win both of these and you're the nominee. Finish second, maybe you have a shot if you can take South Carolina. Third, you've got no chance, especially if you scream like a crazed loon afterward. Iowa and New Hampshire have been the elephant (and donkey) graveyards of the political process.

Why New Hampshire and Iowa, you ask? I don't know. Perhaps it's because they're highly representative of the diverse population that is the United States:

	UNITED STATES	IOWA	NEW HAMPSHIRE
TOTAL POPULATION	299,398,484	2,982,085 (.996% of total U.S. pop.)	1,314,895 (.44% of total U.S. pop.)
% WHITE	80.1%	94.9%	96.1%
% BLACK	12.8%	2.3%	1%
% HISPANIC OR LATINO	14.4%	3.7%	2.2%
% ASIAN	4.3%	1.4%	1.7%
% OF POPULATION THAT DISPLAYS A WEIRD OVERBITE WHEN DANCING	84.4%	96.3%	97.8%

Source: www.census.gov

Okay, obviously that's not it. Let's try again: How is it that two states that collectively represent just over 1% of the country population-wise—two states that are whiter than the crowd at a Jeff Foxworthy concert—have arrived at a position where they practically determine the presidential candidates from our two major parties? Maybe it has something to do with harkening back to the era of our country's founding, when it really *was* all about a handful of white dudes who owned farms deciding what's best for everyone else.

This year, finally, some other states have had enough and decided it's time to crash the Iowa–New Hampshire primary party. Because of this, the classic two-state strategy has suddenly been rendered obsolete.

Or not. At the time of this writing, it's impossible to tell, so in order to cover all bases, this chapter will now split into two divergent paths.

If, in the end, the traditional New Hampshire–Iowa primary dominance held sway, turn to the next page.

If the other states' moving up their primary and caucus dates ended up having a significant influence on events, turn to page 75.

Don't even consider reading both sections; that would be a complete waste of your time, given that only one of them is relevant to your run at the White House.[1]

LONG MAY IOWA AND NEW HAMPSHIRE REIGN!
PRIMARY SCENARIO 1

Regardless of the reasons why, everything is riding on the battle for these two states. Taking heed of legendary former House Speaker Tip O'Neill's maxim that "all politics is local," the first part of this challenge will ask you to demonstrate your knowledge of Iowa and New Hampshire.

Decide whether each statement applies to New Hampshire or Iowa (or one of the other choices … you get the idea).

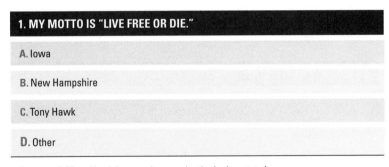

1. MY MOTTO IS "LIVE FREE OR DIE."

A. Iowa

B. New Hampshire

C. Tony Hawk

D. Other

Answer: B (Tony Hawk is a good guess, but he isn't a state.)

---

[1] And given that it's entirely probable that I'll use some of the same gags in both sections.

2. CORN!

A. Iowa

B. New Hampshire

C. A and B

D. A and B, but not C

E. B and D

F. F

Answer: A

3. MY FAMOUS NATIVES INCLUDE MANDY MOORE AND SARAH SILVERMAN.

A. Iowa

B. New Hampshire

C. Hotchickistan

Answer: B or C

4. I WAS THE NINTH STATE ADMITTED TO THE UNION.

A. Iowa

B. New Hampshire

C. It's a trick question. Obviously New Hampshire was admitted before Iowa since it's one of the original colonies, but who would really know or care[2] whether it was the ninth state admitted to the union?

[2] People from New Hampshire, dummy. That's why I'm asking.

D. My head hurts

Answer: B (Minus 3 delegates if you chose D. We've just gotten started and already you have a headache? Typical, always with the headaches, except on our anniversary where you just lay there like some kind of corpse.)

5. THE FIRST AMERICAN IN SPACE WAS BORN HERE.

A. Iowa

B. New Hampshire

C. Another trick question. No one has ever been in space. The entire space program, including the moon landing and the shuttle disasters, is an elaborate hoax designed to allow the government to covertly funnel massive sums of taxpayer dollars into secret research into cloning and shit like that.

Answer: B is the answer for now, but if you do get elected president, and you find out that C is the truth, drop me a line.

6. THE CAPITOL OF IOWA IS _____.

A. Ames

B. Des Moines

C. Iowa City

D. Iowaburg

Answer: I don't know, look it up.

7. THE CAPITAL OF NEW HAMPSHIRE IS _____.

A. Concord

B. Manchester

C. How many people could actually name a third city in New Hampshire?

Answer: A, no B, no A, definitely A

8. IOWA HAS THE THIRD LARGEST WIND-POWER ECONOMY IN THE WORLD, BEHIND:

A. Alaska and Texas

B. California and Texas

C. Holland and Denmark

D. Whogivesashit and Areyoukiddingmeland

Answer: D

9. NEW HAMPSHIRE WAS THE BIRTHPLACE OF WHICH PRESIDENT?

A. John Quincy Adams

B. Josiah Bartlett

C. Franklin Pierce

D. Justin Timberlake

Answer: C

10. NEW HAMPSHIRE WAS THE FIRST STATE TO:

A. Enact a state lottery

B. Embrace same-sex unions without a court order

C. A and B

D. No fucking way—A and B? Seriously? *New Hampshire?* I always thought they were a bunch of tight-asses up there.

Answer: C or D

It's not enough to be well-versed in the basic facts about Iowa and New Hampshire. In order to successfully pander to the electorate, you must be intimately familiar with the issues that concern the voters. For each state, put the following issues in rank order (1–10), from most important to least important.

IOWA

____ War in Iraq

____ War on terror

____ Dislike of Cheeseheads[3]

____ Economy

____ Budget deficit

____ Ethanol

____ Abortion

____ Death penalty

____ Making sure their caucus remains the first contested primary event

____ The record of the University of Iowa Hawkeyes football team

[3] People from Wisconsin who are followers of a particular religious sect know as Packers Fans. They identify themselves by wearing foam or plastic wedges of cheese on their heads. They are additionally identified by the smell of bratwurst.

If you hit my rankings (below) on the head, give yourself **3** points. Deduct **1** point from the maximum **3**-point total for every difference in rank between your answer and the correct one. For example, if you rated Economy first, but it is actually seventh, you'll deduct, let's see … second, third, fourth, fifth, sixth, seventh … **6** points, since that's the difference between **7** and **1**, giving you **–3** points for that issue. Got it? Me neither.

IOWA

1. Making sure their caucus remains the first contested primary event
2. The record of the University of Iowa Hawkeyes football team
3. Ethanol
4. Dislike of Cheeseheads

5–10. All that other shit

NEW HAMPSHIRE

_____ Preserving that rock formation that looks kind of like an old dude's face

_____ Preserving their status as the first primary in the nation

I just realized that those two things are the extent of my knowledge of what the people of New Hampshire might be concerned about, which makes it impossible to fill out a list of ten issues. So instead, I've provided some drawings. One of them is New Hampshire. If you can correctly identify the state, give yourself 24 delegates.

SCREW YOU, IOWA AND NEW HAMPSHIRE!
PRIMARY SCENARIO 2

Any good primary strategy is drawn from former House Speaker Tip O'Neill's maxim that "all politics is local." What primary voters want most of all is to know that you share the specific concerns of their state, and what better way to demonstrate your fealty to their interests than to be intimately familiar with the issues that are most important to citizens of any state? Those are the state slogan, the state bird, and what the state's residents hate the most.

First, state slogans. Try to identify the correct slogan for each of the following states.

1. NEW HAMPSHIRE

A. Kinda Small, But Pretty

B. Get Your Rocks Off in the Granite State

C. You're Going to Love It Here

D. Use a Map; You'll Find Us

E. None of the above

2. IOWA

A. Corn and Stuff

B. Life-Changing

C. Just Corn and Not Much Else

D. Corn

E. A and B

3. SOUTH CAROLINA

A. Smiling Faces. Beautiful Places

B. Yankees, Go Home

C. We've Got Nice Beaches Too, Though You Don't Really Think of Us for That

D. God's Country

E. All of the above

4. FLORIDA

A. Hey, Jews and Old People, It's Very Quiet Here

B. Hurricanes Only Come Every Few Years

C. Golf! Motherfuckers!

D. Visit Florida

E. The Sunshine State

5. MICHIGAN

A. Not as Many Lakes as Minnesota, But Still Lots of Lakes

B. Great Lakes, Great Times; More to See

C. If You Go North, It's Like You're Practically in Canada

D. Cars Used to Be of Some Importance Here

E. Take a Michigander at Us

Give yourself 5 delegates for each correct answer. **1.** C; **2.** B; **3.** A; **4.** D;[4] **5.** B

---

[4] The "Sunshine State" is Florida's nickname, not its slogan. When you are indeed the "Sunshine State," apparently you can get away with a slogan as unimaginative as "Visit Florida."

On to state birds. Many states are justifiably proud of their unique flora and fauna, the native species that set them apart from other states. For this part of the challenge, match the bird to its state.

1.	Illinois	A.	Cardinal
2.	West Virginia	B.	Cardinal
3.	North Carolina	C.	Cardinal
4.	Indiana	D.	Cardinal
5.	Ohio	E.	Cardinal

Give yourself 5 delegates for each correct answer. **1.** D; **2.** B; **3.** C; **4.** A; **5.** E

The last part of our challenge concerns your knowledge of what people in various states hate most. Sympathizing with regional pet peeves is a surefire way to win people over. It creates a bond of trust between you and the voters, reassuring them that you really understand their needs.

It's going to be tougher this time, though. Rather than give you a range of choices for each state, I'm going to make you come up with the answers entirely on your own. It's hard, but I know you can do it.

WHAT DO THEY HATE THE MOST?

1. Utah: _____

2. New Jersey: _____

3. Pennsylvania: _____

4. Wisconsin: _____

5. North Dakota: _____

6. Massachusetts: _____

7. Texas: _____

8. Wyoming: _____

9. Colorado: _____

10. New Mexico: _____

11. Oregon: _____

12. Washington: _____

13. Maryland: _____

14. Idaho: _____

15. Tennessee: _____

16. Delaware: _____

17. South Dakota: _____

18. Nevada: _____

19. Oklahoma: _____

20. Nebraska: _____

21. Minnesota: _____

22. Virginia: _____

You get 10 delegates for each correct answer. **1–13.** Washington politicians; **14.** Homos; **15–22.** Washington politicians

The key, except in Idaho, is to make it clear that despite the fact that you are clearly a politician, you are not one of *those* politicians, the *Washington* kind, who are bad, bad, bad, and you're never going to become one, even when you're elected president.

QUE SERA SERA, THAT'S ALL SHE WROTE, YOU DON'T HAVE TO GO HOME, BUT YOU CAN'T STAY HERE, THAT'S ALL FOLKS: THE PRIMARIES END

Remember just a couple of pages ago when I implied that you were going to continue on your journey through the primaries?

I was lying, because this is it. Primary season is over. Kind of sudden, I know, but that's how it is in primary politics. One day you're a potential president; the next you're dead and buried. Just ask Howard Dean.

To find out if you're still alive, tally your total number of delegates. If my math is correct, you could earn a maximum of 3,000.

If you have 1,500 or more, congratulations! You're your party's nominee to be the next president of the United States. Turn the page to continue the election adventure.

If you have fewer than 1,500 delegates, go join George Smathers in Obscuretown. Population: You (and George Smathers).

Also, step away from the book. As I promised earlier, it will now dissolve into dust. If you'd like to go buy the book again and give the challenges another try, please do so, but this book is, any second now, going to cease to exist.

Stop looking at it. You can't be looking at it when it happens. A watched book never dissolves. Just leave it in the street somewhere; trust me, it's going to blow away in the wind.

GENERAL ELECTION

Congratulations! You've won the nomination of your chosen party. Now the stakes are even higher. If you lose the final showdown or, even worse, lose it badly, or lose it four years in a row (hello, Buffalo Bills[1]), you'll have the word "loser" on your permanent record.

I know this doesn't seem fair since, by and large, you have won more than you have lost, but we are invariably judged by our performance on our largest stage. It's like *American Idol* writ large. Sure, you might dazzle us during the initial audition with your soulful interpretation of "Unchained Melody"—but make it to the finals and botch the words to "Rhythm Is Gonna Get You" on Gloria Estefan night, and you're going to be a national laughingstock.

The good news is that you're now going to have a whole slew of new goodies to play with, like a campaign slogan, campaign bumper stickers, and even a vice-presidential candidate to order around.

The other good news is that the unquestioning love of your political base has now kicked in. This means that in the general election you're trying to grab the voters left in the middle, the undecideds—that 5 to 7 percent of people who refuse to shit or get off the pot. These are the people who are in front of you at Arby's, staring endlessly at the overhead menu, gap-mouthed, with a blank look on their faces as they dither over what to order, even though every asshole on the planet knows that when you go to Arby's, you eat the damn roast beef.

I know, it seems sort of demeaning to have to work so hard to draw these people to your side of the ledger, but it is what it is. If Hillary Clinton can tolerate her husband nailing everything with a vagina in order for her to have a shot at the White House, currying favor with the undecideds is the least you can do.

---

[1] Sorry, Mr. Russert.

I want to take a moment to apologize for all the work I've been making you do. It's rare that a writer will make such rigorous demands of readers, forcing them to answer question after question as they turn each page. I've sprained my brain several times in the writing of the book, so I can only imagine how difficult it must be to read it. In terms of difficulty I'm thinking *So You Want to Be President* is likely to be up there at the top of the history of literature, alongside Joyce's *Finnegans Wake* and *The Princeton Review's Guide to SAT Preparation*.

So I've decided to ease off the accelerator and make this next challenge one you can't possibly lose. Before we get to that, though, let's just relax a bit by looking at this picture of puppies. If you look long enough and allow your eyes to gradually go out of focus, you'll even see a delightful hidden image.

Did you see the hidden image?
Yeah? Really?

No, you didn't. There isn't one. I was just messing with you. What the hell are you doing, taking time out to stare at puppies while your eyes glaze over? We're in the midst of a presidential election! Letting your guard down even for a moment might lead to some sort of catastrophic mistake such as having sex with a hairdresser or being for something before you were against it.

It's time to craft your campaign slogan—your "I Like Ike," your "Tippecanoe and Tyler Too," your "Nixon or Else, and I Mean It!"

Choosing the right slogan is of the utmost importance to your campaign. It's widely believed that Ronald Reagan defeated Jimmy Carter in the 1980 election due to Carter's failed first term and Reagan's movie-star charisma. But the reality is that Reagan won the battle of the slogans, pitting his "Are You Better Off Than You Were Four Years Ago?" against Carter's "It Could Probably Get Worse." For the love of God, Carter made Eeyore look like Tony Robbins!

I learned the lesson of a bad campaign slogan myself during my brief career as a campaign strategist during a different 1980 election. Someone in the Illinois legislature thought it would be fun to allow the state's grade-schoolers to "elect" a state animal. In every school there would be candidates, campaigns, voting, the whole shebang. The contenders were the raccoon, the fox squirrel, the opossum, the red fox, the thirteen-lined ground squirrel, and the white-tailed deer. I was in fifth grade at the time, and I was selected (via the pulling of my name out of a hat) to be campaign manager for the red fox.

Vulpes vulpes, the red fox, a "small, doglike animal" with rusty red fur and "white underparts," wouldn't have been my choice for state animal, but I was determined to see this little guy to victory school- and hopefully statewide.

I had a vision of strength for the state animal of Illinois: an image that represented Chicago, the City of Broad Shoulders, as well as the strong backs of our rural farmers, the feeders of the nation. For my campaign communication centerpiece, I settled on a line drawing of my candidate in its natural woodland habitat, ears up and alert, one foot perched on a log, one of the other candidates—the fox squirrel—limp in its mouth, the slogan in big bold marker[1] at the bottom: "Red Fox—Taking No Prisoners!"

Naturally, I'd made a rookie mistake. I had failed to consider the audience for my message, boys and girls ranging from kindergarten all the way to sixth grade. My portrait of an aggressive carnivore appealed to only a small segment of the constituency, the kids who burned ants with magnifying glasses.[2] Most of the rest of the school was horrified. One first-grader burst into tears when he saw the poster (even though he couldn't read the slogan), crying out, "Why does that one aminal hate the other aminal?" He rolled into a ball, huddled up against the lockers, and shoved his thumb in his mouth. We didn't see him after that. Maybe he transferred.

The opposition pounced on our weakness, digging into the World Book Encyclopedia for some inconvenient truths: red fox, "lethal predator, susceptible to rabies." The opposition turned my slogan against me, turning "Taking No Prisoners" into "Taking Twenty Rabies Shots In Your Stomach If That Nasty Thing Bites You." The red fox was sunk. You can't spin rabies.[3]

We went down to a humiliating defeat to the white-tailed deer, that leaf-eating pussy. It was like choosing John Kerry over Rambo. Disgusting.

Anyway, I'm mostly over it.

The great slogans—"It's Morning in America," "Where's the Beef?" "May the Force Be With You," "You've Got to Fight for

---

[1] I used those markers that were scented like candy. Grape was always my favorite. For the record, it doesn't taste as good as it smells.

[2] Otherwise known as my friends.

[3] Just get in your time machine and ask Howard Dean after his famous post-Iowa meltdown. But don't get too close; he looked contagious.

Your Right to Parrrrtaay," "Eats Lightning, Craps Thunder"—resonate in the public consciousness forever. That's what you're shooting for with your slogan.

The problem is that your slogan needs to be as unique and special as you are, my little candidate snowflake. In a handful of words: It needs to encapsulate your *personal* vision for where you want to take this country of ours.

So, your next challenge is to formulate your campaign slogan. Remember, it should connote strength, resolve, and your willingness to fight for America at home and abroad. Once you have your slogan (one per customer, please), send it to me care of Tow Books at towbooks@gmail.com. I'll evaluate it and tell you how many electoral votes it's worth, up to a maximum of 30.

Now, turn the page for an even funner activity: deciding on your campaign logo!

[INSERT YOUR NAME HERE] FOR PRESIDENT

You and Your Logo

★★

The campaign logo is an often-overlooked factor in presidential elections. An exhaustive analysis of the 2000 and 2004 election results reveals that George W. Bush's victories can be directly attributed to his undoubtedly kick-ass campaign logos:

Strong, powerful, patriotic, forward-looking. I can't stand the guy, and it almost makes *me* want to vote for him.

Let's consider the 2004 election in more depth. By this time, President Bush had already shown himself to be one of the worst presidents in all of history. He was facing off against an experienced politician with a giant head reminiscent of the costumed characters we love so much when we visit Disney World. This, combined with lingering Democratic Party resentment over the outcome of the 2000 election, should have presaged a Kerry landslide.

However, in a misguided effort to capture a youthful image, Kerry made the important tactical error of letting running mate John Edwards's four-year-old son, Jack, design the logo. The direct result of this decision was a logo so ugly, even the most partisan of Democrats refused to put it on their bumpers.

For your campaign, you won't be designing your own logo, but it will be up to you to give final approval. Below I've provided five different logo styles. Choose the best one, and you'll earn yourself ten electoral votes.

Since I don't know your name, I've substituted mine. It's not because I'm on a power trip or anything.

LOGO 1

LOGO 2

LOGO 3

LOGO 4

LOGO 5

YOUR CHOICE: _____

As you should have deduced, the best choice is the strong, powerful, throbbing **LOGO 5**. **LOGO 4** is a reasonably close second, but its imagery is too veiled to really cut through the visual clutter. **LOGO 3** would be effective for reminding people what year it is, but not much else.

LOGO 1, I don't want to talk about.

LOGO 2 is appropriate only if you're running for president of Care Bear Land.

If you did choose **LOGO 5**, give yourself 25 electoral votes.

If you just couldn't decide, I don't know what to do with you.

PLEASED TO MEET YOU ...
AND YOU ... AND YOU

You and Your Handshake

★★

Your handshake is your calling card, your first foot forward *and* your lasting impression. Your handshake can say a lot of things, such as "I overcompensate for my insecurities," "I have a germ phobia," or even "I'm a pirate."[1]

But what your handshake *needs* to say is: "I'm the next president of the United States."

What does *your* handshake say? In order to find out, this chapter's challenge will involve a bit of field work.[2] Before we get to that, though, let's determine your literacy in basic handshake etiquette with a short quiz.

1. A HANDSHAKE IS PERFORMED _____.

A. primarily by highly trained acrobats

B. If you're using "handshake" as a euphemism for masturbation, the answer is: at least once a day; twice on the weekends

---

[1] If instead of a hand, you extend a hook for shaking.

[2] What, you thought you could run for president entirely from your easy chair, or the throne of your own toilet? Maybe if you're Elvis, but unless the *Weekly World News* knows something the rest of us don't, there's no chance that you're Elvis.

C. by balling up your fist and waving it in a menacing way at the asshole who just honked at you because you were fractions of a second too slow in accelerating after the light turned green

D. by wrapping the thumb and fingers of the right hand around the other person's hand, locking thumb webs, gripping to ensure firm palm-to-palm contact, and pumping one to two times

E. by extending the right hand, palm down, fingers slightly parted. As the gentleman comes toward you, he kneels and, while bowing his head, lightly grasps your fingers and plants a kiss on them as light as the brush of a butterfly's wings

F. by completing the action described in D above, followed by clasping at the hilt of the thumbs, then hooking hands together at the fingers only, then simultaneous finger-snaps, and, finally, pantomiming the taking of a "toke" from a marijuana joint

G. By bashing your oversized forearms against those of the other person.

H. None of the above.

2. WHICH OF THE FOLLOWING ARE PROPER OCCASIONS FOR A HANDSHAKE? (CHOOSE ALL THAT APPLY.)

A. At the start of a business meeting

B. When you first meet a baby

C. Right after you've sneezed a wad of snot into your hand

D. Mid-surgery

E. When your spouse returns home from work

F. At the end of a business meeting

G. When offering congratulations on a job well done

H. After reaching agreement over a dispute

G. Following the acceptance of a job offer

I. Upon spotting someone totally minding his own business in a public place who is making it clear by reading a book that he'd rather not be bothered

J. When greeting the alien species that has landed in your backyard

K. When an adorable collie trots up to you, sits down, and raises its paw

L. Post-coitus

Give yourself **+5** electoral votes for each correct answer . **1.** D, unless you are a princess (in which case E is correct), a douchebag (F), or a member of the 1987 Oakland A's (G). **2.** A, D, F, G, H, K, L

See? Just two questions. I promised you the first quiz would be short.

Let's move on to the hard part: the "hands-on"[3] aspect of this challenge. The only way to determine the quality of your handshake is to get out there and shake some hands. In order to quantify the quality of your handshake, your assignment is to shake hands with one hundred non-related people, then ask them to fill out a survey regarding their handshake experience.

Once you have completed one hundred handshakes and one hundred surveys, compile the data to determine how close (or far) you are to (or from) achieving handshake mastery. After the survey form below, you'll find a handy scale that will make it quick and easy to interpret the data, provided you understand regression analysis using standard matrices and the Hoffnagel constant.

Please note that you are authorized to photocopy the following survey form, but as for any other pages in the book, don't even think about it.

---

[3] Oh, I slay me!

HANDSHAKE EXPERIENCE SURVEY

Hello! Welcome to a short survey regarding your handshaking experience with _____. Your opinion is valuable to us—so valuable, in fact, that we are asking for an extremely small amount of your time and offering nothing in return. For each question, mark the choice that best reflects your answer. Please do not just barely glance at this survey and then throw it away, because we have fashioned this paper out of a special material that bursts into flame when it is out of direct contact with light. So for example, if you are in a mall and you throw this sheet into the garbage, the entire contents of the garbage can will ignite, causing a panic. Later, mall security and Vice President Dick Cheney will review the surveillance tapes, and you will be shipped off to a cell at Guantanamo Bay.

Seems like an easy choice: a short survey or a lifetime of detention.

GENDER: ___ Male   ___ Female   ___ Shemale

AGE: _____

EDUCATION

___ Preschool

___ Grade school

___ High school

___ Trade school

___ Some college

___ Some college because I got too into pot and booze first semester, so I had to drop out, but then I invented those things that hold your nose open while you sleep to keep you from snoring, so it doesn't really matter that I didn't graduate from college

___ College degree

___ College degree from an Ivy League school[4]

___ College degree from a "near-Ivy"

___ Postgraduate degree

POLITICAL AFFILIATION

___ Republican

___ Democrat

___ Independent

___ Republican, but I'm saying Independent because I like to preserve the illusion that I'm a free and flexible thinker not beholden to a particular party

___ What the one above says, except substitute Democrat for Republican

1. **ON A SCALE FROM 1 TO 5, WHERE 1 STANDS FOR "I WOULD RATHER HAVE THE FLESH PEELED FROM MY BODY USING A CHEESE GRATER" AND 5 STANDS FOR "I WOULD SAY THE EXPERIENCE WAS AS PLEASURABLE AS THE FIRST TIME I SAW CATHERINE ZETA-JONES ON CELLULOID," HOW WOULD YOU RATE THE HANDSHAKE?**

___ 1 ___ 2 ___ 3 ___ 4 ___ 5

2. **WHICH OF THE FOLLOWING WORDS BEST DESCRIBES THE HANDSHAKE YOU JUST EXPERIENCED? (CHOOSE ONE, IF YOU KNOW WHAT'S GOOD FOR YOU.)**

___ Firm

___ Squishy

___ Moist

___ Slack

___ Painful

___ Spongy

[4] What is with your insistence on always shoehorning that fact into the conversation? Get over it! You're not *that* special.

___ Orgasmic

___ Lackluster

___ Blockbuster

___ Netflixy

3. WHICH LOCATION DO YOU THINK BEST DESCRIBES THE HANDSHAKE YOU JUST EXPERIENCED? (CHOOSE ONE.)

___ The white sand beaches of Barbados

___ The bottom of my junk drawer

___ Martina Navratilova's instep

___ Boston

___ The place in the erectile dysfunction commercials where the couple watch a sunset while sitting in side-by-side bathtubs

___ My mother's womb

___ The underside of a desk in a high-school classroom

4. COMPLETE THIS SENTENCE BY CHOOSING THE PHRASE THAT MOST CLOSE-LY DESCRIBES THE HANDSHAKE YOU EXPERIENCED. IT WAS LIKE _____.

___ standing and waiting extra long for the bus

___ feeling like I'm the third most important person in the room

___ stroking the bloated corpse of a decomposing sturgeon

___ being caressed with the finest velvet

___ coming home again after a short absence, as if I'd popped out to the store for just a minute

___ Christmas and Hanukkah rolled into one

___ Arbor Day and Columbus day rolled into one

___ eating a low-carb turkey wrap

5. WHAT IS YOUR BEST GUESS AS TO THE CURRENT OCCUPATION OF THE PERSON WHOSE HAND YOU JUST SHOOK?

___ Pipefitter

___ College professor

___ Typist

___ President of the United States

___ Ne'er-do-well

___ Roustabout

___ Gadfly

___ Rapscallion

___ Doctor

___ Lawyer

___ Indian chief

___ Actor

___ Actor playing a lawyer on TV

___ Other: _____

Now, tally the results as follows.

STEP 1: Get a big piece of paper.

STEP 2: Get a pencil.

STEP 3: If you got a pen, go back and get a pencil this time. You'll be making mistakes, and you'll need to erase.

STEP 4: For each question, tally the results.

STEP 5: What do you mean, you don't know what that means? It's perfectly clear—TALLY THE RESULTS.

STEP 6: Okay, I'll explain it as I would to a child. At the top of the sheet of paper, for the first question, mark down how many respondents chose each rating. Multiply the number of people who chose the rating by the value of the rating, e.g., if

50 people chose 2, that would result in a value of 100. Add up all the values. Divide the values by 5 for your average rating.

STEP 7: For the second question, tally how many times each of the possible answers was chosen. Put the choices in rank order.

STEPS 8–10: Do the same thing for questions 3–5.

STEP 11: Was that so hard?

STEP 12: Don't answer that. It was a rhetorical question.

---

1. If your average score is **4** or higher, give yourself 5 electoral votes. If you scored an average of **2** or lower, subtract 5 electoral votes and return to your friendless existence. 2. If your top answer is "Firm," **+5** electoral votes. "Orgasmic," **+3**. "Moist," **–2**. All others **+0** electoral votes. 3. If your top answer is either "My mother's womb" or "Martina Navratilova's instep," **+5** electoral votes. If your top answer is "Boston," **–2** All others **+0**. 4. If your top answer is "Eating a low-carb turkey wrap," **+5**. 5. If your top answer is "President of the United States," **+5**.

You now have two things: a gauge of the quality of your handshake, and some sort of communicable disease contracted from shaking hands with so many different people.

You're welcome.

SHIT YOU SHOULD PROBABLY KNOW: PART 1

The Constitution

★★

The Constitution of the United States of America is the greatest do-over[1] of all time. As you should know if you're going to be president, prior to the Constitution, our amalgamation of newly independent colonies was governed by the Articles of Confederation. The Articles were developed and ratified quickly in order to provide a central government during the Revolutionary War but were soon found wanting when it came to light that disputes between states would be solved via "pigg eating" contests[2] in which each state would put forward their "champion" for mano-a-mano porcine ingestion competition. The first "champion" to devour an entire roast pig, asshole to eyeballs, would win the dispute for their state. When it started to look like Randall "The Belly" Wilkerson of Delaware would be able to turn the tiny state into a juggernaut that could essentially veto the desires of every other

---

[1] My own personal experience with do-overs is considerably less positive, including possibly the worst do-over of all time during an epic third-grade-recess kickball game. With the bases loaded and the score tied in the bottom of the 132nd inning (it was a continuous game played all year), I squibbed a weak roller back to the pitcher, only to yell "D-O, D-O!" immediately, claiming an untied shoe. (My shoes were always untied, as I was the last kid in my class to learn how to tie his shoes, which I did at age 23.) After much yelling (the other team) and crying (me), the do-over was granted. Unfortunately, while trying to kick for the fences on the do-over, I whiffed the ball completely, fell, and broke my coccyx.

[2] The annual Nathan's-Hot-Dog-eating contest held every July 4th on Coney Island was born out of this tradition.

---

state, a constitution convention was re-convened to address this and other shortcomings of the Articles.

For the purpose of adjudicating these sorts of issues, the Constitution established a Supreme Court to replace the supreme barbecue. No one is quite sure what happens to settle disputes behind the scenes of the Supreme Court, but we're pretty sure[3] it isn't pig-eating.

The Constitution has remained the centerpiece of our nation's laws ever since its adoption. As a candidate, you're going to need to know it backwards and forwards so you don't accidentally propose a law that directly contradicts our most basic rights, like, say, a program allowing the president to authorize wiretapping of domestic phone calls without judicial authorization or oversight. Certainly any president who did such a thing would be run out of office with a nation of personal-privacy-loving citizens in hot pursuit brandishing pitchforks.

Below, I've scrambled the language of different constitutional amendments. If you really know your Constitution, you'll know which amendment is which, even with the words all mixed up. Label each amendment with its proper number. To increase the difficulty, I've also interspersed a scrambled passage from my seventh-grade science project on the effectiveness of different antacids in neutralizing stomach upset.

CONSTITUTION SCRAMBLE

1. The arms shall not be infringed being necessary to the security of a free State of people to keep the right and a well regulated Militia bear.

2. Except as a punishment neither any involuntary servitude or party nor crime shall exist within the United States the subject place whereof for slavery to their jurisdiction shall have been convicted duly.

---

[3] But not positive.

---

3. Several states regard enumeration census and taxes on incomes to lay and collect the Congress from whatever derived any power source or shall have without to apportionment among the without.

4. Hydrochloric mortar Tums distilled Pepto-Bismol pH materials water pestle acid meter included and ounces three and Rolaids each Maalox and of Mylanta.

5. The United States right of the United States sex on citizens denied or abridged of vote shall to not be by the by or any account state of.

6. Or upon probable cause by oath or affirmation the people to be secure things and to be seized papers, and effects in their persons, houses searches and seizures and no unreasonable warrants shall not be violated shall, issue the right of the persons particularly describing the supported but against the place to be and searched.

You earn 4 electoral votes for each correct identification. (If you mistakenly identified the scrambled passage from my seventh-grade science project as a constitutional amendment, subtract 2 electoral votes.) **1.** The Second Amendment. Gave us the right to wear short sleeves and also to own guns. **2.** The Thirteenth Amendment. Abolished slavery (once we got that whole Civil War thing settled, anyway). **3.** The Sixteenth Amendment. Established the income tax. **4.** My seventh-grade science project. On a scale that went "Outstanding, 1st, 2nd, 3rd," the project earned a "5th." **5.** The Nineteenth Amendment. Gave women the right to vote. Arguably more damaging than the Sixteenth Amendment.[4] **6.** The Fourth Amendment. Established protection from unreasonable searches and seizures, safeguarding porn collections across America (unless there's a warrant).

If you didn't do so well on this quiz, no worries. When your administration ignores the Constitution, you can just use ignorance as an excuse.

[4] Kidding!

I NOW DECLARE YOU RUNNING MATES

Choosing Your Vice President

★★

It's no accident that during the campaign season your vice presidential candidate is referred to as your running "mate," because choosing your running mate shares traits with matrimonial practices from a number of different cultures.

As with Hindus or the Hapsburg Dynasty, a president/vice-president match is often an arranged marriage, a coupling of convenience brought about by outside forces such as party power brokers, the press, and public opinion.

As in the Catholic tradition, you and your running mate are bonded together for life. Your fates are inextricably and permanently intertwined, like Ross and Rachel, only without the sex[1] or the kick-ass apartment.[2]

And like just about every marriage, you and your running mate will enjoy an initial honeymoon period (three, four days) followed by inevitable ups and downs before you settle into a long period of static coexistence until you die.[3]

This is why it's important to conduct more due diligence in choosing a vice-presidential candidate than my buddy Jerry Blach-

---

[1] Probably.

[2] Also probably.

[3] I should note like every marriage except mine, which remains a constantly renewing gift and more than one man could hope for.

101

man did in looking for a life mate, since he found his wife by walk-ing into a bar and shouting, "Is there any woman in here who doesn't think I'm too ugly to love?"

There are, however, important differences between finding a mate and finding a running mate. The first key concept in finding a mate is known as "dating within your league." The second key concept in finding a mate is known as "massive ingestion of alcohol." The third key concept is known as "settling." In sum, the modern partnership is about finding that one acceptable trait that balances all the other horrible faults, as in "He doesn't *always* pop his boils in bed" or, "At least she makes an effort to keep her toenails attractive" or even "He earns only a little below the median household income."

However, when you're choosing a running mate, rather than try-ing to find that one good thing that makes up for the bad, you're looking for "the fatal flaw." History is littered with failed campaigns dragged into the electoral abyss by a vice-presidential albatross.

Consider George McGovern, who chose Terry Eagleton to be his partner on the Democratic ticket only to find out that Eagleton had previously undergone electroshock treatments in order to lose weight. Once the public found out that Eagleton was a closet fatty, he was forced to withdraw, throwing the McGovern campaign into chaos and handing Richard Nixon a return trip to the White House despite the fact that Nixon's hobby was performing petty stick-ups at office buildings.

Or consider Democratic nominee Al Gore, who chose Senator Joe Lieberman as his running mate, not realizing that Lieberman was actually a Republican.

And don't forget the 1992 independent candidate Ross Perot, who was actually leading the two major candidates (President George H.W. Bush and Bill Clinton) in the polls until he selected the Lucky Charms Leprechaun as his number two.[4] The stubborn Perot

---

[4] The vain and egomaniacal Perot wanted to make sure he had a running mate more pipsqueaky than himself.

refused to admit that he'd selected a fictional breakfast-cereal mascot and ultimately could play only spoiler.

Identifying the fatal flaw is the name of the game in the next quiz. On the surface, each of the candidates described below will appear to be a great asset to your campaign. However, all but one of them have a fatal flaw that, by itself, would be enough to kill your chances of winning the election. Choose the right person, and you'll earn yourself twenty-five whole electoral votes. Because I'm not that well versed in current politicians who may make good vice-presidential candidates, I'm going to focus on finding contenders in areas I'm more familiar with. Don't let that bother you; the right running mate is in there, I promise.

RUNNING MATE CHOICE NO. 1

NAME: **Dakota Fanning**
AGE: 14 (but has maturity far beyond her years)
OCCUPATION: Actress
HOME STATE: Georgia
CURRENT RESIDENCE: California

NOTABLE ACHIEVEMENTS
- Has been in, like, *tons* of movies.
- Won an MTV Movie Award.
- All of her permanent teeth have come in.
- Successfully avoided quickie marriage and drug habit (thus far, fingers crossed).

PROS
- Adorable moppet.
- Charisma that lights up the screen.
- Emotional performance ranges from being completely terrified (*War of the Worlds*) to completely cute (*I Am Sam*).
- Room to mature.
- Excellent connections to big potential donors (Tom Cruise, Denzel Washington, Julia Roberts).

CONS
- Celebrity threatens to overshadow your candidacy.

- May long for greater variety of roles than just "Vice President."
- Gets pouty when tired.
- Has yet to go through puberty; could turn out ugly.
- Agent gets 10 percent of all votes.

RUNNING MATE CHOICE NO. 2

NAME: My TiVo
AGE: 5
OCCUPATION: Digital video recorder
HOME STATE: NA
CURRENT RESIDENCE: My living room

NOTABLE ACHIEVEMENTS
- Turned television watching into an "on-demand" activity.
- Eliminated need to watch commercials.
- Name has become a verb, as in, "I TiVo'd *My Super Sweet 16*."

PROS
- Good memory (160 gigabytes).
- Anticipates needs (suggests shows you may like based on viewing patterns).
- Sleek, unobtrusive design.

CONS
- "Bleep ... bleep ... bleep" noise gets annoying after a while.
- Must be plugged into power source.
- Vulnerable to lightning strike.

RUNNING MATE CHOICE NO. 3

NAME: Chocolate cake with vanilla buttercream frosting
AGE: Best eaten within three days of preparation
OCCUPATION: Dessert
HOME STATE: NA
CURRENT RESIDENCE: NA

NOTABLE ACHIEVEMENTS
- Name has become synonymous with something easy, as in "a piece of cake."
- Come on, it's cake, for chrissakes!

PROS
- Delicious.
- Moist.
- Associated with birthdays, which generally are viewed as positive things (at least until you get old, you know, like 40).
- Satisfies those who like both chocolate and vanilla.

CONS
- Contributing factor to diabetes.
- Fattening.
- As crazy as it sounds, some people prefer pie.
- Okay if from a box, but best made from scratch, which is time-consuming.

RUNNING MATE CHOICE NO. 4

NAME: My dog, Oscar
AGE: 3
OCCUPATION: Layabout
HOME STATE: South Carolina
CURRENT RESIDENCE: South Carolina

NOTABLE ACHIEVEMENTS
- House-trained.
- Once got within six or seven feet of a squirrel.
- Repelled postal-carrier invasion by barking.

PROS
- Cute.
- No, seriously, he's really cute. I'm not just saying that because he's my dog. Look—cute!
- Relatable; over half of all U.S. households have dogs.

CONS
- Lacks appeal for sizable cat-lover population segment.
- Communicates only in barks, whines, and tail-wags.
- Desire to hang head out of window of moving car makes him vulnerable to assassination attempts.

RUNNING MATE CHOICE NO. 5

NAME: **Bob Dole**

AGE: 85 (Holy shit! Dole is 85? He's doing pretty damn good for 85.)

OCCUPATION: Former senator

HOME STATE: Kansas

CURRENT RESIDENCE: Washington, D.C.

NOTABLE ACHIEVEMENTS

- Spent twenty-seven years in United States Senate.
- Decorated World War II veteran.
- Republican nominee for president, 1996.
- Republican nominee for vice president, 1976.
- Pepsi spokesperson.

PROS

- Extremely experienced.
- Good relationship with Congress (wife is a Senator).
- Gravitas.

CONS

- Tendency to refer to self in third person is sort of annoying.
- 0 for 2 in national campaigns.
- Apparently suffers from "limp dick."

Review all the potential candidates once more before you make your choice. And again, this is really important. Find the fatal flaw. Done? Okay, now write your choice in the space below in your own blood[5] to seal its permanence.

[5] Not too much blood. We don't want it to seep through the page.

Ready for the answers?

MY DOG, OSCAR: Wrong

Fatal flaw: He's *my* dog, asshole. You can't just go around taking another person's dog and making them your vice presidential running mate. **+0**.

DAKOTA FANNING: Wrong

Fatal flaw: She may help you get elected, but once the general public gets to experience Ms. Fanning in action as vice president, the Articles of Impeachment with your name on them won't be far behind as the nation will clamor for your impish second banana to take over the lead role. As both Presidents Bush have shown us, an unpalatable vice president is great job security.

TIVO: Wrong

Fatal flaw: It's just a glorified VCR; it's nothing to get that excited about, dude. Imagine a campaign appearance with you standing there with your arm flung around a TiVo. Ridiculous. **+0**.

BOB DOLE: Wrong

Fatal flaw: Even Bob Dole knows that Bob Dole is old news. **+0**.

CHOCOLATE CAKE WITH VANILLA BUTTERCREAM FROSTING: Correct

You can never go wrong with cake. If you chose cake—and I can't see how you would've done otherwise—give yourself **35** electoral votes.

THEY LIKE YOU ...
THEY REALLY, REALLY
LIKE YOU!

You and Your
Nominating Convention

B elieve it or not, at one point, political conventions were actually newsworthy. In the early days, primary results were more like suggestions, and the nominee was chosen during the convention itself in smoke-filled back-room deals.[1] Even as late as 1952, Adlai Stevenson was drafted into the nomination from the convention floor despite not having competed in any of the primaries, which really must've sucked for the other guys—at least until Eisenhower mopped the country with Stevenson in the general election, after which Stevenson's Democratic rival Estes Kefauver delivered his famous "Nyah Nyah Nyah" address.

Now, though, political conventions are about as spontaneous as a Ron Popeil infomercial, with the nominee signed and sealed, just like the chicken juices following a forty-five minute turn in the Popeil "set it and forget it" rotisserie. A political convention has become the sales platform to launch a product (you). Your convention needs to be carefully and specifically planned to show off your product (again, you) to maximum effect.

---

[1] In fact, in 1836, Martin Van Buren earned the Democratic nomination when the deliberations were conducted in a room with uncommonly poor ventilation, causing all the party power brokers to pass out and suffocate from the cigar smoke. Van Buren went on to win the general election and became forever known as "President Iron-Lung."

The programming should be safe, predictable, and not too edgy. (You've never seen Ron lop off one of his own fingers with the Veg-O-Matic, have you?) In 1968, a piece of interpretive dance scheduled for the Democratic Convention titled *Police and Love* turned horribly wrong as a bunch of real Chicago cops misinterpreted the performance and thought that hippie-beating season had started. The resulting riot tainted the nomination of Hubert Humphrey, helped usher Richard Nixon into office, and set the contemporary dance movement back decades.

Your challenge this time around is to arrange the programming for maximum effectiveness, effectiveness being synonymous with stultifying boredom punctuated by maybe one decent speech, your acceptance of the nomination, and a shitload of balloons, streamers, and confetti.

The format for the next quiz is borrowed from the logic section of the Law School Admission Test (LSAT). Based on the information provided, schedule the final night of your party's convention in order to launch your official candidacy with minimum chance of conflict and maximum fanfare.

GROUND RULES

1. You must schedule every moment between 8:00 PM and 11:00 PM.

2. Speeches last 20 minutes, except yours, which will go for 40 minutes.

3. Introductions may last either 5 or 10 minutes.

4. All other kinds of appearances last 10 minutes.

5. All speakers must be introduced by someone.

6. You may not schedule two speeches back to back, because even the best speeches are really boring.

7. After your nomination, your chief rival during the primaries will give a speech in order to foster unity, but he refuses to go on directly before you because you're a scumbag who took him out at the knees with anonymous smears about his predilection for Thai hookers.

8. All your grade-school-aged children, grandchildren, nieces, nephews, and captives need to make an appearance by your side in order to humanize you, but if they are up past 10:00, they turn into hell demons.

9. Sister Sledge is just happy to have a gig and will come on stage to sing "We Are Family" at any time.

10. Your spouse must introduce one speaker but may not introduce you because the schedule would be derailed by the extended face-sucking when the two of you greet each other on stage.

11. A distinguished member of the opposite party will give a speech in order to reinforce the message that the other party is loco.

12. A token celebrity must be brought on stage to introduce a speaker because celebrities are usually much better-looking than politicians, and because a celebrity presence will help hold the interest of the television audience, who are missing their favorite shows in order to watch your political infomercial. The token celebrity cannot introduce the chief political rival.

13. In order to take a stab at offering something entertaining, a team of acrobats (some Cirque du Soleil–like shit) will perform. They refuse to perform directly after the appearance of the small children.

14. An ex-president from your party will speak. His talk will take an extra five minutes in order to allow for the standing ovation.

15. An award-winning director has produced an 10-minute campaign film that may or may not be used to introduce your speech.

16. You must leave at least 10 but no more than 15 minutes at the end, during which you stand on stage while balloons and confetti drop from the rafters as you soak up the applause and pretend to acknowledge and wave at people in the crowd.

8:00   9:00

Those are the ground rules; the rest is up to you. Use the timeline below to arrange the events in an appropriate order.

Give yourself **34** electoral votes if your schedule matches this one:

8:00–8:10	Sister Sledge performance
8:10–8:15	Spouse speaker introduction
8:15–8:40	Ex-president speech
8:40–8:50	Small children appearance
8:50–9:00	Token celebrity introduction
9:00–9:20	Member of opposite party speech
9:20–9:25	Vice-presidential candidate introduction
9:25–9:45	Chief primary rival speech
9:45–9:55	Acrobats
9:55–10:05	Award-winning director campaign film
10:15–10:45	Your speech
10:45–11:00	Balloons/confetti/waving

How did you do? If you're thinking there's more than one acceptable solution, you're probably right. You have no idea how time-consuming it was to do this chapter unless you actually did try to reason this out, in which case I question your sanity. If you honestly think your solution is as good as the one provided here, go ahead and take the electoral votes. At this point, I really don't care.

10:00   11:00 end

The Punditocracy. No, it's not the latest cool-kid band out of Brooklyn; it's the name for the collection of talking heads (again, not the band) that clutter our various media outlets. They frequently come in the form of newspaper or magazine opinion columnists (George Will, David Brooks, Maureen Dowd, Joe Klein) who spend their Sundays not in church, but sitting around a table with Tim Russert or George Stephanopoulos.

We also have the political "media personalities." Media personalities tend to be hosts of their own often eponymous television shows. They and the pundits are close cousins, species with many similarities but several key differences—kind of like chimpanzees and orangutans, or Hanson and the Osmonds.

Pundits like to consider themselves "analysts," forming their learned opinions free of ideological bias through a careful study of the candidates, the issues, and the populace, but a truer reflection of where these opinions come from can be found in this illustration.

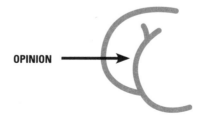

OPINION ———►

Like pundits, media personalities analyze the news and deliver opinions, but instead of presenting an "unbiased"[1] opinion, they rely on a very specific ideological filter that tends to, shall we say, color their versions of events.

The most obvious indication that you're in the presence of a pundit is when, with the utmost confidence and clarity, he or she predicts something that is almost certainly wrong.

One example of a pundit is Thomas Friedman, the Pulitzer Prize–winning columnist for the *New York Times*. At one point he was an incisive commentator on Middle East politics, until an unfortunate accident plunged him in a kind of reverse-*Memento* situation in which he can predict only six months into the future[2]. Here are actual statements Friedman made between 2003 and 2006 on the topic of the Iraq war (emphasis mine).

> "The next **six months** in Iraq—which will determine the prospects for democracy-building there—are the most important six months in U.S. foreign policy in a long, long time." (In a *New York Times* column, 11/30/03)

> "What I absolutely don't understand is just at the moment when we finally have a UN-approved Iraqi caretaker government made up of—I know a lot of these guys—reasonably decent people and more-than-reasonably decent people, everyone wants to declare it's over. I don't get it. It might be over in a week, it might be over in a month, it might be over in **six months**, but what's the rush? Can we let this play out, please?" (On NPR's *Fresh Air*, 6/3/04)

---

[1] Quotation marks included to connote irony. The idea that the average pundit is "unbiased" is about as believable as a multibillionaire Jewish businessman-turned-politician running for president as an Independent with a hope of winning. (Note: If by the time this book reaches your hands there is indeed a President Bloomberg, this joke isn't going to work as well as I expected.)

[2] I'm only speculating that Thomas Friedman suffered some sort of head trauma, but I can't come up with a better explanation.

"What we're gonna find out, Bob, in the next **six to nine months**, is whether we have liberated a country or uncorked a civil war." (On CBS's *Face the Nation*, 10/3/04)

"I think we're in the end game now. ... I think we're in a **six-month** window here where it's going to become very clear and this is all going to pre-empt, I think, the next congressional election—that's my own feeling— let alone the presidential one." (On NBC's *Meet the Press*, 9/25/05)

"I think that we're going to know after **six to nine months** whether this project has any chance of succeeding—in which case I think the American people as a whole will want to play it out— or whether it really is a fool's errand." (On *The Oprah Winfrey Show*, 1/23/06)

"Well, I think that we're going to find out, Chris, in the next year to **six months**—probably sooner—whether a decent outcome is possible there, and I think we're going to have to just let this play out." (On MSNBC's *Hardball With Chris Matthews*, 5/11/06)

How can someone who has so often been so wrong continue to be given column inches in the most influential paper in the country? Who cares? What's important is that, despite the average pundit being about as accurate at predicting the future as a Ouija board at a ten-year-old girl's slumber party, the punditocracy often drives the public debate on a candidate.

In many cases, pundits' misguided analyses even become conventional wisdom. How else would we know that Al Gore is dull, Ronald Reagan was sleepy, and Hillary Clinton wants to turn the country into a feminist commie paradise where all men sacrifice their testicles at the altar of Athena when they turn eighteen?

I know, it makes my head hurt too, which is why I'm writing a book about how to run for president, rather than running for president.[3]

The easiest way for you to tell that you're in the presence of a "media personality" is by the really crazy shit that is spewing out of his or her mouth. For this chapter's exercise, your challenge is to identify some media personalities by correctly guessing which personality is spewing which brand of crazy shit.

We're going to borrow our format from the classic game show *Name That Tune*. For each personality, I will give you five different phrases that represent his or her particular brand of opinion-making. After reading *each* phrase, try to guess who the media personality might be. After the list of phrases, I will provide the correct answer.[4] If you were able to guess the personality correctly after just one clue, give yourself 5 electoral votes. If it took two clues, you earn 4 electoral votes, and so on down to 0 electoral votes if you are unable to successfully identify the personality even after all the help I've given you, which is pretty ungrateful if you ask me.

MYSTERY PERSONALITY NO. 1

1. "God gave us the Earth. We have dominion over the plants, the animals, the trees. God said, 'Earth is yours. Take it. Rape it. It's yours.'"

   YOUR GUESS _____

2. "I think the government should be spying on all Arabs, engaging in torture as a televised spectator sport, dropping daisy-cutters wantonly throughout the Middle East, and sending liberals to Guantanamo."

   YOUR GUESS _____

3. "These broads are millionaires, lionized on TV and in articles about them, reveling in their status as celebrities and stalked by grief-arazzis. ... These self-obsessed women seemed genuinely unaware that 9/11 was an attack on our nation and acted as if the

---

[3] Well, because of that and the fact that as soon as some reporter asked *me* if I've ever inhaled, I'd have to say, "Do you want the list alphabetically or chronologically?" (Note to Mom: Just kidding.)

[4] Probably.

terrorist attacks happened only to them. ... I've never seen people enjoying their husbands' deaths so much."

YOUR GUESS_____

4. "My only regret with Timothy McVeigh is he did not go to the *New York Times* building."

YOUR GUESS_____

5. "We should invade their countries, kill their leaders, and convert them to Christianity."

NAME THAT PERSONALITY_____

CORRECT ANSWER: **Ann Coulter.** Okay, that was an easy one—the nuttiest of the nutty, the sluttiest of the slutty, the least deserving of continuing to draw breath of those who continue to draw breath.

MYSTERY PERSONALITY NO. 2

1. "That's my advice to all homosexuals, whether they're in the Boy Scouts, or in the Army or in high school: Shut up, don't tell anybody what you do; your life will be a lot easier."

YOUR GUESS_____

2. "Shut up!" ... "Pinhead!"

YOUR GUESS_____

3. "You must know the difference between dissent from the Iraq war and the war on terror and undermining it. And any American that undermines that war, with our soldiers in the field, or undermines the war on terror, with 3,000 dead on 9/11, is a traitor. Everybody got it? Dissent, fine; undermining, you're a traitor. Got it? So, all those clowns over at the liberal radio network, we could incarcerate them immediately. Will you have that done, please? Send over the FBI and just put them in chains, because they, you know, they're undermining everything and they don't care, couldn't care less."

YOUR GUESS_____

4. "I am not going to let oppressive, totalitarian, anti-Christian forces in this country diminish and denigrate the holiday and the celebration."

YOUR GUESS_____

5. "Yeah, I'm obnoxious, yeah, I cut people off, yeah, I'm rude. You know why? Because you're busy."

NAME THAT PERSONALITY_____

CORRECT ANSWER: **Bill O'Reilly.** Also pretty easy, since there's only one man who holds equal hatred for homosexuals, Democrats, and people who say "Happy holidays."

MYSTERY PERSONALITY NO. 3

1. "Look, let me put it to you this way: the NFL all too often looks like a game between the Bloods and the Crips without any weapons. There, I said it."

    YOUR GUESS _____

2. "When a gay person turns his back on you, it is anything but an insult; it's an invitation."

    YOUR GUESS _____

3. "I'm doing what I was born to do. That's host. You're doing what you were born to do. That's listen. Together, we make a heck of a team."

    YOUR GUESS _____

4. "Feminism was established to allow unattractive women easier access to the mainstream of society."

    YOUR GUESS _____

5. "I am addicted to prescription pain medication."

    NAME THAT PERSONALITY _____

CORRECT ANSWER: **Rush Limbaugh.** Duh.

MYSTERY PERSONALITY NO. 4

1. I'll tell you who should be tortured and killed at Guantanamo: every filthy Democrat in the U.S. Congress."

    YOUR GUESS _____

2. "Is it [that] you hate this president or that you hate America?"

    YOUR GUESS _____

3. "[Democrats should] stay home on Election Day ... for the sake of the nation."

    YOUR GUESS _____

4. "It doesn't say anywhere in the Constitution this idea of the separation of church and state."

    YOUR GUESS _____

5. "Can we pray for the re-election of George Bush?"

NAME THAT PERSONALITY _____

CORRECT ANSWER: **Sean Hannity.** That one was tougher. Think of Sean Hannity as Rush Limbaugh without the drug habit.

MYSTERY PERSONALITY NO. 5

1. "Just because your voice reaches halfway around the world doesn't mean you are wiser than when it reached only to the end of the bar."

   YOUR GUESS _____

2. "We must not confuse dissent with disloyalty. When the loyal opposition dies, I think the soul of America dies with it."

   YOUR GUESS _____

3. "To be persuasive we must be believable; to be believable we must be credible; to be credible we must be truthful."

   YOUR GUESS _____

4. "Our major obligation is not to mistake slogans for solutions."

   YOUR GUESS _____

5. "Good night, and good luck."

   NAME THAT PERSONALITY _____

CORRECT ANSWER: **David Strathairn** playing the fictional character **Edward R. Murrow.** I understand there's some confusion over this point; some people mistakenly believe Clooney's award-winning film *Good Night, and Good Luck* is a biographical film of a real person. But just look at those quotes: "not confuse dissent with disloyalty"? Credibility built on truth, of all things? If that's not fantasy, I don't know what the word means.

THE DIRT OF YOUR ENEMY IS YOUR VICTORY SOAP

You and Opposition Research

Opposition research is the secret ops of political campaigning—the cloak and dagger, the black bag, the Bourne Identity. It's a trip through the filth of your opponent's life in an effort to find his Achilles' heel and leak it to the press in order to cause lasting and permanent damage to his candidacy.

I know … kind of exciting, isn't it?

Opposition research is how we found out that George W. Bush got cited for driving under the influence, Al Gore didn't really invent the Internet, and Ronald Reagan had a jellybean fetish, and it's powerful, powerful stuff.

While the other chapters in the book are mere exercises designed to test your presidential mettle in hypothetical ways, this time you're going to get have to get your hands dirty—because that's just how opposition research rolls.

Remember, everyone has something to hide. The deeper you dig, the more dirt you uncover. Here's just a short list of some of the things to look for in your opponent's life:

    Sexual deviancy

    Tax evasion

    Littering

    Failure to send thank-you notes for wedding gifts

119

Drinking and driving

Not recycling

Ripping the tags off of mattresses

Poor tipping

Software piracy

Cow tipping

Actual high seas piracy

Petty theft

Undercooking poultry

Alcohol addiction

Unrevealed sex change

Dungeons & Dragons dungeon master

Employing undocumented workers

Benefiting from a sweetheart land deal

Drug addiction

Actual dungeon, dungeon master

Insider trading

Soap opera addiction

Tardiness

Throwing out child's baseball trading cards

Not wearing shower shoes at the gym despite having athlete's foot

Spacing out in line at the bank when it's his turn to step up to the counter so the teller has to say "next" over and over again

Saying "a whole 'nother"

Attempting to initiate "the wave" at sporting events

And many more.

Let's get down to the business of wrecking someone's life.

STEP ONE: TARGETING

Since you are only hypothetically running for president, your first step is to choose an opponent to target with your research. Go to your community's White Pages and pick a name at random.

WRITE THE NAME IN THIS SPACE: _____

This is now your chief rival for the White House. You will do anything to stop him or her from being victorious. Remember, this individual is evil and wishes to undermine whatever way of life you in your infinite wisdom know is best for America and Americans, and Armenians for that matter.

STEP TWO: DIGGING

Now that you have an opponent, do everything you can to learn as much as you can about the darkest corners of his or her life. You're allowed to use any method you can think of as long as you don't get caught. If you do get caught, e-mail me at towbooks@gmail.com, and I'll send you the "Campaign Cover-Up Challenge" to complete.

Not sure where to start looking for dirt? Just ask yourself: "What would I be mortally embarrassed about if people found out about it?" Here's an illustration.

1. Go to your computer. Type in **www.google.com**.
2. In the search box, type **John Warner + country music**. Among the results will be a link to an article I wrote extolling the virtues of the country-pop group Rascal Flatts.
3. Please don't read the article, no matter how much you'd like to.
4. After all I've done for you, you can't do me the little favor of steering clear of an article in which I declare that Rascal Flatts is "toe-tapping?"
5. I hate you.

Let's see if this qualifies as opposition research on me.

First, is this embarrassing? Yes.

Have I tried desperately to get the editors of the Web site where the article was published to remove it? Of course.

Do I know why I would publicly praise one of the cheesiest groups to hit the music scene in the last thirty years? I do not.

Do they have potentially even more embarrassing information about me that allows them to strong-arm me into leaving the article up for display to anyone in the world with an Internet connection so it will continue to shame me for all eternity, or at least until an electromagnetic pulse from a rogue nuke plunges our entire society back into a pre-industrial age?[1] I'm not saying.

Do I still occasionally listen to the album in question? Once again, I'm not saying.

Anyway, this isn't about me. This is about your newfound, phone-book-picked rival. It's time to do some digging.

Your tools are not limited to Google. Feel free to break into your opponent's house, copy the contents of his hard drive, stalk him over a period of weeks, interrogate his friends and family, steal his trash, kidnap his pets, sleep with his spouse, or do anything else that might yield information such as Social Security number, mother's maiden name, bank account numbers, credit score, Krugerrands, two-for-one coupons on liquid Tide, or anything of that ilk.

STEP THREE: SEND TO ME FOR EVALUATION

When you're done, send it to me c/o the publisher. I will comb through the material and evaluate its usefulness as campaign leverage, and send you a full report along with the number of electoral votes you've earned for this challenge (up to a maximum of forty).

You can expect a reply in six to eight ... [2]

---

[1] Something I almost look forward to every time I go back and read the article.

[2] Decades.

YOU DIDN'T DO ALL THAT YOURSELF, DID YOU?

You Are Not a Crook (But Your Cronies Should Be)

The previous chapter was a test: a test of your ability to think quickly and clearly as a leader. If you did any of the things I discussed in the last chapter, you have failed that test, and I can definitively declare that you do not have what it takes to be President of the United States.

Succeeding at politics for sure requires that hands get dirty, but they should never be *your* hands.[1] The sort of opposition research described in the last chapter should always be done by subordinates, ones who can be trusted to keep their mouths shut and remind you to turn off your secret office-taping system before you give them their orders.

If you weren't fooled by my little challenge, go ahead and get someone else to complete the opposition research for you. Try Karl Rove. I hear he's available these days.

---

[1] Unless you're doing a Habitat for Humanity photo op or some crap like that.

SHIT YOU SHOULD PROBABLY KNOW, PART II

The Concerns of Everyday People Who Are Nothing Like You

Q uick—answer these five questions. Knowing the correct answer to one of them is absolutely vital to winning the presidency. But which one?

1. At the dissolution of the Ottoman Empire following World War I, which new countries were created?[1]
2. What is the maximum range of a Gulfstream IV jet?[2]
3. What is Sporty Spice's real name?[3]
4. What is the average price of a gallon of milk in the United States[4]?
5. If you are experiencing a burning sensation during urination, and by burning I mean the feeling that diamond-tipped razor blades are being scraped along the inside of your urethra, which disease should you suspect first?[5]

All important questions for sure, but when you're surrounded by a phalanx of reporters who are salivating at the chance to record your

---

[1] There are actually forty of them, including Albania, Hungary, Iraq, Jordan, and the like.

[2] 5,800 miles.

[3] Rosemary Gatorade.

[4] See below; I'm planning to recycle this question.

[5] The clap (other acceptable answers: VD, gonorrhea), not that I'd know anything about it.

next gaffe for all posterity, only a wrong answer to question four has the potential to brand you as out of touch with the concerns of regular Janes and Joes, thus rendering you instantly unelectable.

Don't believe me? The popular historical explanation for the implosion of Gary Hart's 1988 Democratic campaign was the release of tabloid photos showing the comely Donna Rice perched on his lap during a yachting trip. However, as we later found out during the Clinton presidency, only a few tight-ass Republicans care about whether the president gets a little extracurricular trim. No, the reason for Hart's collapse was his answer to a reporter's question very similar to number four above:

> **REPORTER** Congressman Hart, can you tell us the average price of a gallon of gas?

The correct answer (at the time) was around $1.10. But let's see what Congressman Hart had to say:

> **GARY HART** Who gives a rat's ass? I'm about to blow off some steam with some world-class poontang.

With that one botched answer, Hart instantly went from front-runner to also-ran (though an also-ran who allegedly had sex with Donna Rice, who you have to admit *was* hot in that '80s kind of way).

Anyhoo, during slow periods in the campaign, the media will enjoy springing these sorts of questions on you in order to generate a story. It's crucial not to fall into the trap of looking out of touch with the electorate, so I've provided a quiz that will alert you to shortfalls in your familiarity with the concerns of ordinary Americans. Yes, I know, they're unwashed and have incomes under $50,000, but they also have the right to vote, so don't skip this.

Scoring instructions will follow each section of the quiz. The first section is multiple choice.

1. THE AVERAGE COST OF A GALLON OF MILK IN THE U.S. IS _____.

A. $1.00

B. between $3.50 and $4.00

C. Why buy the cow when you can get the milk for free, knowmsayin?

D. None of the above.

2. THE AVERAGE MARRIED COUPLE HAS SEXUAL INTERCOURSE HOW MANY TIMES PER WEEK?

A. Once.

B. Per week? Try per month.

C. Per month? Try per year.

D. I'd rather not talk about it.

3. DO I LOOK FAT IN THESE JEANS?

A. Of course not.

B. My mother should go blind if I'm lying; no!

C. Honestly? No.

D. I could never lie to you. So, no.

4. IF YOU ACCIDENTALLY FIND A STASH OF POT IN YOUR TEENAGE CHILD'S ROOM, THE BEST COURSE OF ACTION IS TO _____.

A. directly confront him with pamphlets and shit like that that show marijuana will rot your brain

B. tell him to stop bogarting the weed

C. make him take bong hits until he's so sick of getting high that he'll never want to do drugs again

D. introduce him to a bootleg tape of The Grateful Dead's performance of "Dark Star" from that '71 Fillmore West show

5. WHEN YOU'RE SITTING ON YOUR COUCH AFTER A LONG, GRUELING DAY OF WORK, IDLY FLIPPING THROUGH CHANNELS, AND IN A FLASH OF INSIGHT YOU RECOGNIZE THAT YOU'RE JUST TRYING TO NARCOTIZE YOURSELF TO AVOID CONTEMPLATING HOW TRULY INSIGNIFICANT YOUR ENTIRE EXISTENCE IS AND THAT SOMEDAY YOU'RE GOING TO DIE, AND THEN THE PRICKLES INVADE ALL YOUR LIMBS AS THE DARKNESS OF DESPAIR CLOSES IN, WHAT SHOULD YOU DO?

A. Drink.

B. Drink heavily.

C. Drink until you black out.

D. Watch *America's Funniest Videos*; it's always a spirit-salver.

Give yourself **3** electoral votes for each question you answered correctly. **1. B; 2. D; 3. Any of the above; 4. None of the above; 5. D.**

This next part is true or false. Choose the appropriate answer. No, you can't choose two simultaneously, "you know, depending." Lay off your kid's weed.

6. THE DAYTONA 500 IS 500 MILES LONG.	True	False
7. THE DAYTONA 500 IS HELD IN MILAN, ITALY.	True	False
8. DALE EARNHARDT JR. WON A NOBEL PRIZE.	True	False

9. IF DALE EARNHARDT JR. HASN'T WON A NOBEL PRIZE, HE SHOULD.

                                                                                          True   False

10. SCREW THE NOBEL PRIZE—THERE'S RACING ON!   True   False

Give yourself **3** electoral votes for each question you answered correctly. **6.** True; **7.** False; **8.** False; **9.** True (the Nobel Prize for Extreme Coolness); **10.** True

Next: Analogies. Fill in each blank with the word you feel completes each analogy the most successfully.

11. CARRIE BRADSHAW IS TO SARAH JESSICA PARKER AS _____ ARE TO BARRY BONDS.

12. GUINNESS IS TO BEER AS _____ IS TO PISS.

13. EXCITEMENT IS TO THE SUPER BOWL AS CRUSHING BOREDOM IS TO _____.

14. MEDIA ATTENTION IS TO PARIS HILTON AS _____ IS TO A CRACK ADDICT.

15. LEBRON JAMES IS TO MICHAEL JORDAN AS _____ IS TO *HAPPY DAYS*.

Give yourself **3** electoral votes for each correct answer. **11.** steroids[6] **12.** Miller Lite[7] **13.** soccer[8] **14.** crack[9] **15.** Joanie Loves Chachi[10]

That's enough about the lives of common Americans. I'm sure you're getting skeeved out just thinking about such things. Let's roll your campaign bus out of the trailer park and get on our way to 1600 Pennsylvania Avenue.

---

[6] Steroids made Barry Bonds's career in the same way the role of Carrie Bradshaw made Sarah Jessica Parker's.

[7] Guinness is an exemplar of a fine beer; Miller Lite is an exemplar of urine.

[8] The logic here is obvious.

[9] Ditto.

[10] Anyone who thinks LeBron holds a candle to Jordan needs to re-watch their "best of Jordan" DVDs. I'm happy to loan out mine.

POLLING, POLLING, POLLING ... KEEP THOSE SURVEYS ROLLING

Public Opinion Polling

Knock, knock!
Who's there?
Politician.
Politician who?
All politicians are slaves to polls.

The more a politician claims that he doesn't pay attention to polls the more certain you can be that he won't take a crap without a sample of likely voters telling him whether he should use single or double ply to wipe.

Bill Clinton was famous for calibrating his policies to public opinion out of a deep-seated need for approval that can be only partially salved by sleeping with everything with two X chromosomes. President George W. Bush has been equally beholden to polls, though in the reverse way: He's sought to govern in near-perfect opposition to public opinion out of his deep-seated need to look tough because he resents his father's success and his domineering mother's overbearing presence.

As a candidate, you're going to be bombarded constantly by polling data. But just as polls giveth, they can taketh away. With all the polls floating around out there, some are bound not to go your way, and a few of those could actually cripple your candidacy.

You must be ready to counteract and discredit any information that doesn't break in your favor. That's what we're going to practice now. Read this mystery story, inserting your name into the blanks as you go. If you can solve the mystery along with Detective Polly Tix, you'll earn 45 electoral votes!

THE CASE OF THE DISTRAUGHT CANDIDATE

Detective Polly Tix eased back in her chair, threw her shapely legs onto her desk, and opened the drawer where the whiskey lived. It had been a rough week in a series of rough weeks for the private dick. Polly specialized in cases involving elections and campaigns, and for awhile it had seemed like, when one ended, the next began.

As she poured two fingers' worth into a glass, Polly dreamed of November, when, barring a "Florida 2000" situation, she'd finally get a break for at least a couple of months. But what's a girl to do when she's the best and someone's willing to pony up the green-backs for her services?

Just as she'd finished the glass and begun to nod off to sleep right there in the chair, the door rattled and (Your Name) entered. You didn't need to be a great detective to know this person was the frontrunner in the current presidential race, but (he/she) looked nothing like a future president, standing in front of Polly's desk wringing (his/her) hands and looking haggard and harried.

"I need your help, Ms. Tix," (he/she) said.

Polly Tix swung her legs to the floor and sighed while rubbing her fists into her eyes. "Let me guess," she said. "There's a rampant rumor about you doing something grotesque, either advocating for raising income taxes on the middle class, or having sex with barn-yard animals."

"Both, actually," (Your Name), replied, tears forming in (his/her) eyes. "How did you know, anyway, have you heard them?"

"I've heard everything many times before, sweetheart," Polly Tix said, standing and coming around the desk to throw a consoling arm around (Your Name). "Now, tell me what you know."

"The only thing we've been able to find is this press release about the results of a new poll." (Your Name) handed several sheets of paper over to Polly Tix, who quickly scanned the headline: "For immediate release: 60% of those surveyed believe that (Your Name) is a tax-raising goat-fucker."

Polly Tix winced as she leafed through the materials. "That is pretty harsh. Bestiality *and* tax and spending. Ouch."

"I know," (Your Name) cried. "It's going to ruin my entire campaign unless I can discredit the results, but as we all know, polls are totally reliable as an accurate reflector of public opinion. What am I going to do?"

Polly Tix frowned down at the pages, quickly scanning the press release summary, looking for clues.

"According to a recent poll, nearly two-thirds of all those surveyed believe that (Your Name) may have had sex with goats and also wishes to raise taxes on the middle class. Eighty-five percent of those surveyed indicated that knowing a candidate has had sex with goats would make them less likely to vote for that candidate. Ninety-nine percent of those surveyed said they would be less likely to vote for a candidate who had pledged to raise taxes on the middle class."

(Your Name) slumped in a chair, crying softly into (his/her) hands. "We've done some of our own polling and those numbers seem to hold up. Somehow, somewhere, people are getting the idea that I'm a tax-raising goat fucker."

"Well?" Polly Tix said, raising an eyebrow.

"Well what?" (Your Name) replied.

"*Are* you a tax-raising goat fucker?"

"What? Of course not!"

Polly looked long and hard at (Your Name). She'd seen some tax-raising goat fuckers in her day, and (Your Name) appeared to be telling the truth.

Polly had some ideas on where this stuff might be coming from, but first she had to get rid of the sniveling mess in the office so she could hit the pavement and scare up some information. "I'll take the case. Now you just get on home and leave this to me," Polly said, patting (Your Name)'s back reassuringly.

"What's this going to cost?" (he/she) asked without looking up.

Polly mused. Normally she just extracted a tidy monetary sum from her clients, but she'd been following the race and had a good feeling about this candidate's chances, alleged tax-raising goat fucker or no. Suddenly she had a vision for how to get out the detective biz, once and for all, to go to a place with sun and sand, and where the whiskey was mixed into colorful frozen drinks.

"How about making me Ambassador to Tahiti if you win," she said.

The candidate stood up and smiled for the first time since (he'd/she'd) arrived. "That's it? I thought you were going to ask for something big, like Secretary of State or a guest night in the Lincoln Bedroom." The two shook hands and the candidate left, leaving Polly just a moment to look longingly back at the desk chair before heading out into the night.

* * *

Polly stamped her stilettoed heel onto the '92 Trans Am accelerator and thundered out of her parking lot as she headed towards Muck Research. Muck was a marketing research company run by Cameron (Cam) Paine Muck, a sleazy operator willing to whore out his call center to the highest bidder, and a practitioner of notoriously unsound survey methodologies. Polly had known Cam since college, when she'd busted him trying to copy off her answers on an advanced statistics final. She knew that if she was going to prove that (Your Name) was a victim of underhanded actions, she was going to need to find the source of the tax-raising goat fucker rumors, and she had a hunch that Muck Research was the place to start.

She was almost going to enjoy this one.

As she approached the building she cut the engine and lights and used the emergency brake to ease to a silent stop. The building was dark, deserted. It took Polly seconds to pick the front lock, and she was soon inside, using a penlight to guide her towards Muck's office. She extracted a blackjack from her purse just in case she ran into an unexpected visitor during her unexpected visit.

She listened at the office door for Cam Muck briefly before entering and sitting at his desk in front of the computer. She expertly clicked through the files before opening one labeled gfckr.doc. Double-clicking the icon, the document opened on the screen, and Polly read what looked to be the text for a telephone survey:

SAMPLE: 50,000 HOUSEHOLDS WITHOUT PARTY AFFILIATION

Question 1: If you found out that (Your Name) had a plan to raise taxes on middle-income households, would that make you:
  A. Much more likely to vote for (Your Name)
  B. More likely to vote for (Your Name)
  C. Neither more nor less likely to vote for (Your Name)
  D. Less likely to vote for (Your Name)
  E. Much less likely to vote for (Your Name)

Question 2: If it were revealed that (Your Name) enjoyed having sexual intercourse with goats, would that make you:

    A. Much more likely to vote for (Your Name)
    B. More likely to vote for (Your Name)
    C. Neither more nor less likely to vote for (Your Name)
    D. Less likely to vote for (Your Name)
    E. Much less likely to vote for (Your Name)

Question 3: Do you think (Your Name) sounds like a degenerate who isn't fit for pubic office?
    A. Yes
    B. Definitely
    C. Absolutely
    D. Positively
    E. No doubt about it

Question 4: Now, go tell everyone in your neighborhood that (Your Name) is a sexual deviant who is going to raise your taxes.

Question 5: The survey is over. Go on, spread the word: (Your Name) is a tax-raising goatfucker.

Just as Polly read the final sentence, she heard a noise in the hallway. Snapping into action, she hit "print" snatched the pages from Muck's printer, and cracked open the door to the hallway. She saw a flashlight beam sweeping the floor and walls and heard the thump of a nightstick against the guard's thigh just a few feet away. Quietly, she held her breath as she folded the printed pages and tucked them in her ample cleavage. She could smell the guard's after shave, an Aqua Velva man. She had all the evidence she needed. If she could just get out of the building.

    Faster than words, her mind's eye visualized a plan for clobbering the guard from behind. But before she could make the first move, the guard moved off down the hall, whistling as he walked.

Polly slipped out and down the hall, one perfect ankle flashing in the moonlight as she exited the building, hopped back into the Trans, and roared home, her raven hair blowing in the wind.

* * *

(Your Name) arrived at Polly's office early the next day, looking only slightly better than the night before. Polly typed rapid-fire on the keyboard, smiling as she spoke. "Have a seat, Cow(boy/girl); I've got something show you." She stopped typing long enough to hand (Your Name) the printouts from Muck's computer. "I'm just shopping for swimsuits here so I'm properly outfitted for my new job."

(Your Name) looked at the printouts. "Looks like a standard survey to me."

"Look again, numbnuts," Polly said, still smiling, but a little icily. "Maybe I was wrong about you. If you can't figure it out, I'm not sure you're cut out to lead the free world."

* * *

You're up. Within the survey text itself, there are four clues that mark it as the work of someone who isn't interested in a scientifically rigorous and valid survey result. You must name them in order to expose Cam Paine Muck's sinister plan to discredit you as a tax-raising goat fucker.

CLUE 1:

CLUE 2:

CLUE 3:

CLUE 4:

If you found all four of these clues, you get **45** electoral votes.

CLUE 1: The first clue is that 50,000 interviews is far more than necessary for an actual public opinion survey. 400 would do the trick; any more wouldn't be cost-effective. There's only one reason for a pollster to interview that many people: to spread rumors.

CLUE 2: Survey questions 1 and 2 engage in classic "push polling," in which untrue information is put forth in a question as though it is true, thus sowing the seeds of rumor, i.e., "Are you familiar with so-and-so's wife-beating conviction? If so, through which media outlet did you first hear of it?"

CLUE 3: The choices for survey question 3 allow the respondent to answer only in the affirmative. A good survey captures the full range of public opinion.

CLUE 4: Survey questions 4 and 5 aren't actually questions.

How'd you do? Did you earn your 45 electoral votes, getting one step closer to victory and allowing Polly Tix to live out her dream life as a diplomat in a Polynesian paradise?

You'd better hope so. Polly carries a gun, and she really wants that ambassadorship.

DODGE, BOB, AND WEAVE
The Third Rails of Politics

I n politics, as in life, there are some things people will do anything to avoid talking about.

For example, in my life, I would be loath to discuss the time during summer camp when I was seven years old and it had been awhile since I'd had a haircut, so I was maybe a bit shaggy, and we were riding the bus to the swimming pool and one of the older kids (ten at least! I think he had a mustache!) decided he couldn't tell if I was a girl or a boy, so he asked the rest of the bus (probably rhetorically), "Hey, is this kid a girl or a boy?" Before anyone could answer, he declared, "I think he's a girl," then leaned his face into mine and began chanting, "Girl! Girl! Girl! Girl!" while pumping his fist in the air, and soon the whole bus is chanting, "Girl! Girl! Girl!" and anyway, it's not like I still remember this episode so vividly that I have an anxiety attack every time a school bus passes by, and I don't want to talk about it anyway.

Just as I prefer not to discuss my early emasculation at the hands of a grade-school bully abetted by a bus full of cruel children, you need to stay away from "third rail" political topics during your ride down the campaign trail. "Third rail" refers to the electrified subway track, which legend has it will kill you if you urinate on it. I suppose if you touch it, too, but for some reason the dead guys—

137

and it's always guys, because what woman would be so stupid as to try to take a leak on a metal bar with God knows how many volts flowing through it?—are always pissing on it.

Anyway, there are certain topics you just want to steer clear of. Third-rail topics tend to be either (a) intractable problems, e.g., Social Security, or (b) issues that historically and inevitably divide along partisan lines with no acceptable middle ground between them, e.g., the issue that shall not be named.[1]

The cruel, cruel irony is that these are the issues everyone seems to want something done about and everybody wants to talk about, but since nobody can agree on them, if you say anything of substance, you're bound to piss someone off either by sounding too extreme, which alienates the all-important moderates, or by sounding too moderate, which risks irritating the base.

So, it's important to learn techniques for assuring that, any time you are grilled about "third rail" issues, by the time you're done with your answer the voters won't even remember the question.

Third-rail topics tend to take center stage in the debates because the news anchors who moderate the debates are glory-seekers who want nothing more than to stuff a failed candidate's hide and mount it on their office wall.

In this challenge, I will be providing hypothetical answers to debate questions concerning these difficult topics. Each answer contains language that should never be uttered by a presidential candidate, or at least not by one interested in winning. Your job is to cross out the language that doesn't belong, leaving behind an appropriately meaningless, noncontroversial statement.

TOPIC: GLOBAL WARMING

Honestly, anyone who doesn't think that human beings are a pestilence that's slowly or not so slowly strangling the planet has his

---

[1] Abortion.

head up his ass, so my administration will take aggressive steps to limit the emissions of greenhouse gases by doing everything possible, except for taking away your trucks with hemi engines because everyone loves a hemi.

TOPIC: SOCIAL SECURITY

I believe this to be a grave and gathering threat because when you talk about Social Security, you're talking about money that millions of people are going to depend on for food and shelter in their old age, and if we fail to shore up the system, we're going to have a real crisis on our hands, and we're going to have a nation of homeless old people eating canned cat food, which isn't as tasty as it looks. I promise to examine this issue thoroughly and establish a way forward that solves this dilemma once and for all so we can guarantee a happy and secure existence for all Americans in their twilight years.

TOPIC: ABORTION

This is an issue that has divided the country for better than a generation, and it currently divides me from my opponent. But in those divisions there is strength, as we can work together and listen to each other's views in order to reach across that divide and find common ground that allows us to heal the wounds caused by such difficult issues.

TOPIC: HEALTH CARE

When you get sick, you want to get well, and everyone should have the opportunity to have access to the people and services that will help them get well. Like Advil. That always makes me feel better when I have a headache, or even a fever, and it even works on menstrual cramps, though I guess Midol might be better for that stuff, but to tell you the truth, I'm not sure of the difference between Advil and Midol. It could just be a packaging thing. Also, there's too much paperwork and it's confusing. Someone should do something about that.

TOPIC: THE ISRAELI/PALESTINIAN CONFLICT

I've got to be honest, I don't know what the hell to do about that situation. It seems like everyone should just sit down and try to figure stuff out and stop killing each other, but we've tried that many times before. It's like everyone's gone crazy or something. Also, my administration will conduct muscular diplomacy and demand results.

Award yourself **10** electoral votes for each correct answer—and yes, your answer needs to match mine exactly. This is a presidential campaign, not a charity. "Close" counts only in horseshoes and hand grenades.

GLOBAL WARMING

~~Honestly, anyone who doesn't think that human beings are a pestilence that's slowly or not so slowly strangling the planet has his head up his ass, so~~ m[M]y administration will take ~~aggressive~~ steps to limit the emissions of greenhouse gases[.]~~, by doing everything possible, except for taking away your trucks with hemi engines because~~ e[E]veryone loves a hemi.

This amended answer pays lip service to both environmentalists and people who like to drive noisy trucks.

SOCIAL SECURITY

~~I believe this to be a grave and gathering threat because when you talk about Social Security, you're talking about money that millions of people are going to depend on for food and shelter in their old age, and if we fail to shore up the system we're going to have a real crisis on her hands and we're going to have a nation of homeless old people eating canned cat food, which isn't as tasty as it looks.~~ I promise to examine this issue ~~thoroughly and establish a way forward that~~

*solves this dilemma once and for all so we can guarantee a happy and
secure existence for all Americans in their twilight years.*

This answer commits to nothing and leaves you in a position to
take the only action that makes political sense when it comes to Social Security: punting it down the field to the next guy.

ABORTION

*This is an issue that has divided the country for better than a gen-
eration, and it currently divides me from my opponent. But in those
divisions there is strength, as we can work together and listen to
each other's views in order to reach across that divide and find common ground that allows us to heal the wounds caused by such difficult issues.*

When the topic is abortion, it's best to let your surrogates do all
the talking. Everyone knows where the two parties stand anyway.
If you're asked about abortion during a debate, just stare into the
camera and smile until your time is up.

HEALTH CARE

*When you get sick, you want to get well, and everyone should have
the opportunity to have access to the people and services that will
help them get well. Like* Advil *That always* makes me feel better
when I have a headache *or even a fever, and it even works on menstrual cramps, though I guess Midol might be better for that stuff,
but to tell you the truth, I'm not sure of the difference between Advil and Midol. It could just be a packaging thing. Also, there's too
much paperwork and it's confusing. Someone should do something
about that.*

It's simple, it's non-controversial, and it also plants the seed for a
post-presidency endorsement deal.

ISRAELI/PALESTINIAN CONFLICT

~~I've got to be honest, I don't know what the hell to do about that~~ ~~situation. It seems like everyone should just sit down and try to fig-~~ ~~ure stuff out and stop killing each other, but we've tried that many~~ ~~times before. It's like everyone's gone crazy or something. Also,~~ m[M]y administration will conduct muscular diplomacy ~~and de-~~ ~~mand results.~~

You'll do something, just like every other president, but let's not expect miracles—because doesn't that seem like what it's going to take? Promising results would brand you a loon.

SORRY SEEMS TO BE THE HARDEST WORD

Cleaning Up Your Mistakes

★★★

It's inevitable that at some point during your campaign you will make a mistake: a verbal gaffe, a botched policy explanation, a stray mono-digital salutation.[1]

Back in the days when news traveled by mule train, it was no big deal if you made an error. For example, Abraham Lincoln, as he was swinging an axe for a sketch op the day before the 1860 election, accidentally decapitated one of his aides. It took weeks for this news to travel across and through the nation, and by the time it became widely known, Lincoln had already won.

Unfortunately, in this age of technology, where everyone with a cell phone and computer is a mini media mogul, it's impossible to keep a mistake like this under wraps. Just look at all the celebrities who have accidentally taped themselves having sex. Nothing is safe or sacred these days.

Numerous candidates have been undone by their mistakes, some even prior to the YouTube revolution. The examples are legendary:

> Senator George Allen was shown the door by his constituents after his "Macaca moment," when he uttered a racial slur while wearing a Confederate-flag jumpsuit.

---

[1] If you know what I'm saying.

143

During the 1980 election, Jimmy Carter, trying to create an image of a compassionate man who cares about the poor, accidentally hugged a homeless man to death.

In 2004, John Kerry inadvertently revealed his struggle with multiple personality disorder when he declared that he'd voted for war funding before he voted against it.

Mistakes are inevitable, but proper cleanup can limit the damage. Think of serial murderer Jeffrey Dahmer. If he'd been more careful about controlling the fetid stench of rotting, hacked-up corpses, he might still be in business. Granted, politics is a bit messier than ritualized killing, but you get the idea.

The key to a successful political apology is to apologize without apologizing. The Nixon administration pioneered the practice by referring to the Watergate cover-up with the legendary "mistakes were made" construction. Bill Clinton raised it to an art form by redefining the word *is*. George W. Bush has further refined the practice of the non-apology by issuing an executive order banishing mistakes outright.

Here are some illustrations of effective use of the non-apology apology, using events more mundane than seeking to undermine the democratic process.

SQUEEZING THE TOOTHPASTE FROM THE MIDDLE OF THE TUBE
"It's unfortunate that some of the toothpaste has been wasted and the top is too crusted to be screwed back on, but we're looking forward to a future of bright, white, cavity-free teeth."

SLEEPING WITH A PROSTITUTE
"It is regrettable that a sum was paid in return for sexual gratification."

DRINKING DIRECTLY FROM THE ORANGE JUICE CARTON
Under ideal circumstances, a glass is utilized, but that was not the case here.

As you can see, the most effective "apology" puts blame where it belongs: somewhere else.

Following is a challenge to train you in crafting an appropriate public statement following a typical campaign misstep. Let's say you have been caught on an open microphone referring to your opponent as a "half-retarded doofus." The uproar came immediately from your opponent's supporters as well as from the AETH-RD (Americans for the Ethical Treatment of Half-Retarded Doofuses). The media, always up for a circus, has fanned the flames, and now everyone and his mother (and even your mother) is clamoring for a "response."

I've written your response for you, except that at crucial junctures, you must pick the best word or phrase from the choices I give you. Your goal is to say little and signify nothing while urging the campaign conversation to move elsewhere.

You approach the podium and **(A) do the robot (B) nod solemnly to several parts of the room (C) make a raise-the-roof gesture while shouting, "Candidate in da house! Whoop-whoop!"** Your speech begins.

Good evening, **(A) my fellow Americans (B) worthless bitches (C) ridiculous people who can't take a joke.** I come to you today to **(A) jerk you around a bit (B) discuss recent events (C) throw myself at your mercy.** It has come to my attention that some **(A) recent remarks I made (B) stuff you weren't supposed to hear (C) words** have **(A) been revealed to be basically true (B) upset some wusses who, I reiterate, can't take a joke (C) possibly caused offense.** I would like to take this opportunity to **(A) open up a can of verbal whup-ass on each and every one of you (B) speak about this issue (C) withdraw from the race because I can't believe the sort of bullshit I have to put up with to run for president.**

In life, **(A) sometimes unfortunate things happen (B) some people are born doofuses (C) there are events,** and it falls upon us who wish to lead to **(A) tap-dance around the truth (B) take a good, hard look (C) make like nothing happened** so that we may **(A) move forward (B) take stock (C) talk endlessly about the same old crap** and **(A) wallow in self-pity (B) accept the consequences of our actions (C) solve the problems Americans care about.**

So I want to thank **(A) you worthless pukes (B) my fellow Americans (C) the people of Earth** for bringing this issue into the light so we may **(A) get on with the business of**

demonstrating our vision for America (B) finally make it clear that my opponent is indeed a half-retarded doofus (C) stop wasting time on this trivial issue.

Thank you, good night, and may God bless **(A) me (B) the Chicago Cubs (C) America.**

Give yourself **2** electoral votes for each one you got right.

You approach the podium and (B) nod solemnly to several parts of the room. Your speech begins.

Good evening, (A) my fellow Americans. I come to you today (B) to discuss recent events. It has come to my attention that some (C) words have (C) possibly caused offense. I would like to take this opportunity (B) to speak about this issue.

In life, (C) there are events, and it falls upon us who wish to lead to (B) take a good, hard look so that we may (A) move forward and (C) solve the problems Americans care about.

So I want to thank (B) my fellow Americans for bringing this issue into the light (A) so we may get on with the business of demonstrating our vision for America.

Thank you, good night, and may God bless (C) America.

As you can see, the result is a masterpiece of misdirection. It's not clear who did what to whom or why, which is exactly where you want to be.

When in doubt, remember that apologizing and taking responsibility is for the weak. Deflecting blame and refusing to acknowledge wrongdoing are crucial leadership qualities for anyone who wants to be elected resident of the United States, not to mention indispensable survival tools once you're in office.

ONE NATION UNDER GOD

You and Religion

Almost fifty years after John F. Kennedy was forced to declare that the Pope wouldn't be riding shotgun on his administration we've arrived at George W. Bush, who has apparently let Jesus take the wheel of his presidency.

In today's electoral climate, you'll need to chart a course somewhere in between those two extremes. The nation as a whole might be reaching the point where it has had enough of presidents surrendering the big decisions to a higher power, but that doesn't mean we're ready for a bunch of druids presiding over a ritual wolverine slaughter at the inaugural ball.

So, put away your pentagrams and your Ouija board. Pry the Darwin logo from the back of the car, stop the blood-guzzling, and cease all lesbian experimentation,[1] because from now on, you definitely believe in God.[2]

But not too much. Too much is scary. This time around, too much is going to be overboard. You need to negotiate the fine line between saint and sinner,[3] and you're going to use the Ten Commandments as your compass. The root of the word *commandment*

---

[1] Unless you'd like to film it and send it to me.

[2] Let's be clear that we're talking about "God" god, here, the dude with the long beard and white robes who's friends with Santa Claus.

[3] Or Jimmy Carter and Bill Clinton, if you will.

is *command*, which in Latin means "starting point for negotiation." As we've all experienced, the Ten Commandments are not so much rules as guidelines, or, in some cases, not even so much guidelines as suggestions.

As always, it's the exception that proves the rule (or the suggestion), so your job here is to correctly match each Commandment to its acceptable exception. You will use all the exceptions. All commandments will have at least one exception; some will have more than one.

THE TEN COMMANDMENTS

1. I am the Lord thy God, and thou shalt have no other gods before me.
2. Thou shalt not make for thyself an idol.
3. Thou shalt not use the Lord's name in vain.
4. Remember the Sabbath and keep it holy.
5. Honor thy Mother and Father.
6. Thou shalt not murder.
7. Thou shalt not commit adultery.
8. Thou shalt not steal.
9. Thou shalt not bear false witness.
10. Thou shalt not covet thy neighbor's wife.

EXCEPTIONS

A. Not including Kelly Clarkson
B. Unless you drop a hammer on your foot
C. Unless they fail to cater to your every need, because that's the least you deserve
D. Except if you're the government and you're pretty sure the person is guilty
E. Unless you're trying to avoid perjury charges for lying to a grand jury
F. Except for the Ronnie James Dio years, because he sucks compared to Ozzy
G. Except for money
H. Unless it happens in Vegas

I. Except for music, which should be free

J. Unless she is Shakira

K. Or Salma Hayek

L. Or 1960s Ann-Margret

You earn **1** electoral vote for each correct match. **1.** G; **2.** A; **3.** B; **4.** F; **5.** C; **6.** D; **7.** H; **8.** I; **9.** E; **10.** J, K, L

Another difficult balancing act when it comes to religion and public political life is the question of when and where it's okay to invoke God in the public sphere. Fortunately, our founding fathers came up with a handy guideline, also known as the First Amendment:

> "Congress shall make no law respecting an establishment of religion, or prohibiting the free exercise thereof; or abridging the freedom of speech, or of the press; or the right of the people peaceably to assemble, and to petition the Government for a redress of grievances."

Ignore that second part; let's concentrate on the first. As best I can tell, what they're saying is, when it comes to religion, the government is neutral, and for everyone else, it's live and let live, which I guess explains why Scientology gets a tax break.

Below are various scenarios in daily life where God and/or religion may come into play. For each one, you must choose whether the invoking of God and/or religion is "kosher" or "traif"[4] based on the rights invoked in the First Amendment.

1. Thanking God after hitting the winning shot in the NBA finals
    Kosher   Traif

2. Being forced[5] to say the Pledge of Allegiance in a public school
    Kosher   Traif

---

[4] Not kosher, i.e., eating more than your share of pizza is "traif."

[5] Under threat of severe noogie.

3. Thanking God during your Academy Award acceptance speech
   Kosher   Traif

4. Printing "In God We Trust" on U.S. currency
   Kosher   Traif

5. A locker-room prayer before the high-school state championship football game in which the coach says, "Lord, give us the strength to grind their dicks into the dirt and stomp their spines"
   Kosher   Traif

6. Tattooing a Bible verse on one's body
   Kosher   Traif

7. Praying for the New York Yankees to lose
   Kosher   Traif

8. Displaying a nativity scene on the lawn of a church
   Kosher   Traif

9. Displaying a nativity scene on the lawn of a City Council building
   Kosher   Traif

10. Displaying a nativity scene in your pants
   Kosher   Traif

Each correct answer is worth **2** electoral votes. **1. Kosher.** (Lame, but legally allowable.) **2. Traif.** (Invoking God in the pledge is a voluntary exercise in a public school, no matter how much the other kids might stare at you when you're the only one sitting down, or even if the teacher tells you it doesn't really matter how you did on the homework since you'll be spending eternity roasting in hellfire.) **3. Kosher.** (See 1.) **4. Kosher.** (Allowable, since you can insert your own God.) **5. Kosher.** (Silly, but legally allowable.) **6. Kosher.** (See 5 and 1.) **7. Kosher.** (Actually mandatory for residents of Massachusetts.) **8. Kosher. 9. Traif.** (Unless it's part of a Christmahanukwanza display.) **10. Kosher.** (But yuck.)

Turn the page for your next challenge. Do not pass go; do not collect $200.[6]

---

[6] Unless you're willing to disclose it on your campaign finance statement.

When it comes to issues like the economy or the environment, the president has about as much control as a rodeo cowboy has over a bucking bull, or as Britney Spears over her sanity. With those kinds of issues, it's just best to hold on and hope that you don't get your skull caved in or sire two babies with an over-tattooed no-talent.

However, when it comes to conducting foreign policy, the president has significant power. Pretty much alone, you get to decide who's been bad and who's been good, then punish or reward them accordingly. You're like Santa Claus, except with favorable trade policies instead of gifts, and an ultra-high-tech, superiorly trained killing machine instead of coal.

So it stands to reason that you need to know a thing or two about other countries of the world. That thing or two needs to extend beyond the fact that hash and hookers are legal in Amsterdam and Corona is Mexican beer. Don't get me wrong: you don't need to know *too* much. Just the basics—enough so that, when one of your cabinet secretaries mentions unrest in Kazakhstan, you won't reply, "Gesundheit!"

Your first challenge in this section will be whether or not you can distinguish the outline of a foreign country from that of a common

American traffic sign. For each question, simply circle the correct answer. If you'd like to take a shot at naming any of the actual countries, be my guest, but don't think that makes you special, because it doesn't.

1.

A. Foreign country   B. Street sign

2.

A. Foreign country   B. Street sign

3.

A. Foreign country   B. Street sign

4.

A. Foreign country   B. Street sign

 5.

A. Foreign country   B. Street sign   C. Double quarter-pounder with cheese

Give yourself 1 electoral vote for each correct answer. **1. B.** street sign; **2. A.** Foreign country; **3. A.** Foreign country; **4. B.** Street sign; **5. C.** Double quarter-pounder with cheese

Now it's going to get a little tougher. Part of your job as president will be to meet with foreign heads of state. But can you tell the difference between a foreign leader and a foodstuff? It would be pretty embarrassing to ask someone to pass the Sarkozy (instead of the succotash) at a state dinner and inadvertently cause the Secret Service to lift the French Prime Minister and carry him over to you. Each of the names below represents either a foreign leader or food. For each of the following, circle the correct answer.

1. Rahmon
     A. Foreign leader   **B.** Food

2. Ramen

    A. Foreign leader   **B.** Food

3. Al Thani

    A. Foreign leader   **B.** Food

4. Prince Albert

    A. Foreign leader   **B.** Food

5. Ho-Ho

    A. Foreign leader   **B.** Food

6. Hu

    A. Foreign leader   **B.** Food

7. Elizabeth II

    A. Foreign leader   **B.** Food   **C.** Cruise ship

8. Bongo

    A. Foreign leader   **B.** Food

9. Soup

    A. Foreign leader   **B.** Food   **C.** Both

10. Willis

    A. Foreign leader   **B.** Food

Give yourself **1** electoral vote for each correct answer. **1. A.** Foreign leader. Emomalii Rahmon, President of Tajikistan. **2. B.** Food. Dehydrated noodles beloved by college students. **3. A.** Foreign leader. Hamad bin Khalifa Al-Thani, Emir of Qatar. **4. Both.** Head of state of Monaco and brand of tobacco, which some people do eat … accidentally. **5. B.** Food. Delicious chocolate-and-cream snack cake. **6. A.** Foreign leader. (Hu Jintao, President, People's Republic of China.) **7. A.** Foreign leader and **C.** cruise ship. (Queen Elizabeth II, ceremonial head of state, Great Britain; luxury liner with its own casino and disco.) **8. A.** Foreign leader. (Omar Bongo, President of Gabon.) **9. B.** Food. (Nutritious and hot, except for gazpacho, which is cold.) **10. A.** Foreign leader. (Victor Willis, lead singer of the Village People.)

When you're dealing with foreign leaders, one key disadvantage you're likely to have is that they all speak English (quite possibly better than you do), whereas the best you'll be able to do in their language is ask where the bathroom is. Because of this, it's quite possible that when they're out of earshot of your translator, they'll be able to insult you to your face. That's the kind of stuff that shows up on YouTube and makes you look dumber than you really are.

To test your knowledge of foreign languages, I've provided a series of non-English phrases. Some are perfectly acceptable pleasantries, appropriate for any diplomatic occasion. Others are rank insults that would warrant the response of dropping a low-yield nuke on a medium-sized city. For each phrase, circle "Pleasantry" or "Insult."

1. Votre mère a élevé un débile. (French)
   A. Pleasantry   B. Insult

2. Gracias por su hospitalidad y estas cabras también. (Spanish)
   A. Pleasantry   B. Insult

3. Diese person ist so stumm wie eine wanne faule fische. (German)
   A. Pleasantry   B. Insult

4. Zegen u voor het laten van me bij uw vrouw staren juggs. (Dutch)
   A. Pleasantry   B. Insult

5. Maggio le nostre due nazioni per sempre sono amici con i benefici. (Italian)
   A. Pleasantry   B. Insult

Give yourself 1 electoral vote for each correct answer. **1. B.** Your mother raised a real moron. **2. A.** Thank you for your hospitality and these goats as well. **3. B.** This person is as dumb as a bucket of rotten fish. **4. A.** Bless you for letting me stare at your wife's juggs. **5. A.** May our two nations forever be friends with benefits.

Thus ends our foreign relations challenge. Just remember: If and when you are president, don't take any shit, because we are indeed the world's only superpower and we can basically do whatever we want. Think of the world as a giant junior-high lunchroom and the United States as that one kid who matured a little sooner than everyone else (early muscular development, pubes, that kind of thing) and who, therefore, was able to take other people's juice boxes (i.e., natural resources) if he really wanted to.

Didn't everyone always love him? Same thing goes for foreign policy. Diplomacy is just another way of saying "asking for a chocolate swirly."

GO NEGATIVE OR GO HOME

You and Your Last, Best Hope

A s you can tell by the rapidly diminishing number of pages remaining, we're in the home stretch. How do you think you're doing?

Don't answer! It doesn't matter, because we're about to employ the weapon that has the potential to turn around any campaign no matter how poorly it might be going.

That weapon? Negative advertising.

I know, we all hate it. It's causing the downfall of our society, we'd never be fooled by such transparent nonsense, right?

Wrong.

Put simply, negative advertising works. At some point, you'll have to take the gloves off and slap them across the face of your opponent, old-school dueling-style. As anyone who has stood in front of a high-speed fan while someone dumps a bucket of manure into the blades can tell you, "Shit sticks."

Negative advertising worked for Lyndon Johnson. No one who saw it could forget his famous "Daisy Girl" ad, in which he implied that his opponent, Barry Goldwater, advocated dropping atomic bombs on small girls who liked flowers. Going negative also worked for Harry Truman. During his hotly contested 1948 campaign against Thomas Dewey, Truman's supporters placed print ads in major magazines and newspapers implying that Dewey was a sexual deviant (the well-known "Dewey Likes to Have Sex With Little Boys" ad).

Now, you've got to be subtle about it. Nobody is going to believe that a three-times-wounded, Bronze-star-winning Vietnam War hero actually faked it all just so he could brag about his combat experience as he runs for president thirty-plus years later.

Also don't forget that, by law, at some point in the commercial the candidate must stare blankly into the camera and say, "My name is [your name here], and I approved this message," which means exactly that: *You* approved that message.

Which brings us to this chapter's challenge. As the candidate, your job isn't to write copy, but to give the thumbs-up or thumbs-down[1] to the ads your crack campaign team creates. Below, I've given you four scripts for hypothetical negative ads. Choose the one you think will inflict the most damage on your opponent without causing "blowback."[2] Choose correctly, and you will be rewarded with maximum electoral votes. Choose the wrong one (or ones—

---

[1] If you are running for president and have no thumbs, you will be at a serious disadvantage, not just in your ability to signal decisions but in your ability to communicate nonverbally that things are going just swell. Imagine being introduced at a campaign stop, leaping onto the stage and, wearing your biggest smile, shoving two thumbless fists at the audience like some kind of Rock 'em Sock 'em Robot. Not pretty. Not a winning image. So, if you are among the nation's thumbless, I recommend that you have your big toes surgically transplanted to where your thumbs ought (or used) to be. It will look a little funny, but you'll adjust. If you do follow my advice, just remember not to campaign in sandals.

[2] "Blowback" is a colloquial term meaning "unintended negative consequences to oneself." Most people believe the term originated in the military to describe the potential of explosives to harm one's own troops, but that is only partially true. The term is military in origin, but it has been traced specifically to one James Blowback, a corporal in the U.S. Army during World War I, whose lactose intolerance (even powdered milk was a problem) often caused him to visit his gastric distress on his trench-mates, who suspected Corporal Blowback was actually a form of chemical warfare perpetrated by the Germans.

I'm tricky that way), and you may see electoral votes flow into your opponent's column.

(For illustration purposes, we're going to give your hypothetical opponent a nondescript name, Herman Q. Asscrack. He's a United States Senator.)

NEGATIVE ADVERTISEMENT NO. 1: POINT BREAKING POINT

INT. BANK—DAY

A group of **GUNMEN** (who are wearing rubber masks bearing your opponent's likeness and wielding automatic weapons) bursts into a bank, yelling at the customers to get on their bleeping knees. The customers yell hysterically as the gunmen spray bullets into the ceiling and manhandle people to the ground.

CUT TO:

CUSTOMER 1, lying on his stomach on the floor, looks up at **MAIN GUNMAN**.

CUSTOMER 1 (terrified)
> *Please, Senator Asscrack. Haven't you grabbed enough of my money with your tax-and-spend votes in Congress already?*

GUNMAN 1 presses the muzzle of his weapon into **CUSTOMER 1**'s cheek.

GUNMAN 1 (cackling fiendishly)
> *Enough? There's never enough!*

CUT TO:

CUSTOMER 2 climbing to her knees, then being pistol-whipped back to the ground by **GUNMAN 2**.

CUSTOMER 2 clutches at her bleeding head wound.

CUSTOMER 2 (wailing)

> *At least use our hard-earned money to pay off the national debt or strengthen our military readiness!*

GUNMAN 2 delivers a second blow to **CUSTOMER 2**, knocking her completely unconscious. **GUNMAN 3** joins **GUNMAN 2** to lift **CUSTOMER 2** off the ground. Together, they hold her upside down and shake coins out of her pockets.

CUT TO:

GUNMAN 1 jumping up on the counter and unleashing another hail of bullets into the ceiling.

GUNMAN 1 (cackling even more fiendishly)

> *Ha! I'll use it for whatever I want to! I may just build giant golden statues of myself and adorn them in precious rubies and diamonds.*

FREEZE FRAME:

CANDIDATE walks into scene. The entire background remains frozen.

CANDIDATE (oozing gravitas)

> *Unlike my opponent, I've pledged not to use your tax dollars to build giant golden statues of myself.*

CANDIDATE walks over to still-frozen **GUNMAN 1** standing on the counter and jumps twelve feet in the air, delivering a spinning roundhouse kick Matrix-style to **GUNMAN 1**'s head, shattering it into a million pieces.

CANDIDATE turns to address the camera.

CANDIDATE

> *My name is [insert your name here], and I definitely approved this message.*

CUT TO:

CANDIDATE rushes into hospital room and, with eyes closed, places hands on **PATIENT**'s chest. **PATIENT** jerks back to life. **CANDIDATE** turns to face the camera.

CANDIDATE:

My name is [insert your name here], and I approved this message.

PATIENT sits up in bed, smiles and shakes **CANDIDATE**'s hand.

NEGATIVE ADVERTISEMENT NO. 4: GASLIGHT ACTION NEWS

INT. TELEVISION NEWS STUDIO

A **NEWS ANCHOR** sits at the anchor desk. A graphic of Herman Q. Asscrack is over her shoulder.

NEWS ANCHOR (with a mix of Walter Cronkite's authority and Marilyn Monroe's coquettishness)

*Welcome back. Next, we go to reporter **JAMES SANDERSON** who has been out gathering the impressions of regular people, who clearly aren't paid actors unable to find work in legitimate television, film, or even advertising, about presidential candidate Herman Q. Asscrack. James?*

CUT TO:

EXT. CITY STREET—DAY

JAMES ANDERSON stands in front of **AVERAGE AMERICAN WOMAN** while holding a microphone.

JAMES SANDERSON

I'm here with an average American woman to ask her about her impressions of Herman Q. Asscrack. So, average American woman, what do you think of Herman Q. Asscrack?

AVERAGE AMERICAN WOMAN
Who? Never heard of him.

JAMES SANDERSON
He's a senator, and he's running for president.

AVERAGE AMERICAN WOMAN
Nope, doesn't ring a bell. Is this one of those prank shows? I don't have time for this crap.

AVERAGE AMERICAN WOMAN moves on; **JAMES SANDERSON** intercepts **AVERAGE AMERICAN MAN.**

JAMES SANDERSON
Excuse me, sir—what are your thoughts on Herman Q. Asscrack?

AVERAGE AMERICAN MAN (slightly confused)
My colon therapist? Why are you asking about my colon therapist?

JAMES SANDERSON
Never mind.

AVERAGE AMERICAN MAN moves on and **JAMES SANDERSON** intercepts **WOMAN WITH SPECTACULAR BREASTS.**

JAMES SANDERSON
Excuse me, Miss, but can I ask you what you think of Herman Q. Asscrack?

WOMAN WITH SPECTACULAR BREASTS (excitedly)
He's my all-time favorite character from The Chronicles of Narnia!

JAMES SANDERSON
Thank you, Miss.

JAMES SANDERSON turns back to face the camera.

JAMES SANDERSON

> *Well, it looks to me like no one can agree on exactly who Herman Q. Asscrack is. Now, back to the studio.*

CUT TO:

INT. NEWS STUDIO

NEWS ANCHOR back in the studio, looking into the camera.

NEWS ANCHOR

> *Thanks, James; very interesting. It appears that, whoever Herman Q. Asscrack is, he isn't running for president, so it would be pretty silly to vote for him.*

CUT TO: CANDIDATE standing in a field of tall grass, scratching behind the ear of a Labrador retriever.

CANDIDATE (presidentially)

> *My name is [insert your name here], and I approved this message.*

Choose which ad you think would be most effective, and write its title here:[3] _____

Negative advertisement no. 4, "Gaslight Action News": **–20** electoral votes. This ad is, as they say, too clever by half. In theory, it might seem reasonable to issue an ad that tries to convince the electorate that your opponent doesn't exist. But in reality, this is a risky proposition, particularly when the ad repeats his name so many times, which will increase the name recognition of "Herman Q. Asscrack," whoever he is. Even if you are able to convince a sizable number of voters that Herman Q. Asscrack is not a presidential candidate, when they find themselves in the voting booth and see his name on the ballot, many will choose him, just out of a kind of "Huh, I've heard of him" reflex.

Negative advertisement no. 2, "Foreign Film": **+0** electoral votes. While the message at the core of this ad (that Asscrack is both pretentious and fruity) is sound, mimicking a foreign

---

[3] Do it in pen so you're not tempted to change it once you see the correct answer. Go ahead, you own the book, right? It's not like doing the entire crossword puzzle in an in-flight magazine, so when the poor bastard who sits in the same seat on the next flight turns to some word puzzle fun in order to alleviate the boredom of a two-hour delay, he has nothing to do.

film will have every halfway-normal person switching the channel instantly, dropping your ad into the same viewerless abyss as an Andy Richter sitcom.[4]

Negative advertisement no. 1, "Point Breaking Point": +15 electoral votes. This ad effectively draws a distinction between you (heroic; capable of stopping time and leaping fifteen to twenty feet in the air to deliver a devastating death blow) and your opponent (evil, greedy) in terms that voters can easily grasp. The action-sequence nature of the ad will get attention, and the message that you're both an ass-kicker and fiscally responsible will resonate strongly with voters. However, there is a segment of society that seems to identify with charismatic villains with delusions of grandeur—the ones who think the best part of *Silence of the Lambs* is Hannibal Lecter. In addition, some Americans apparently respond to a strongman-style president, and you run the risk of burnishing Asscrack's image in the minds of those voters.

On the whole, this ad would be a positive for you, but it's not worth maximum points.

Negative advertisement no. 3, "Angel of No Mercy": +40 electoral votes. This is the kind of ad that could help tip the balance in a close election. Unlike "Point Breaking Point," this ad portrays your opponent as a weasely sneak, while implying that you have the power to raise the dead (a very difficult proposition) and, by implication, that you will be able to fix our nation's health care system (a likely impossible proposition).

---

[4] Let the record reflect that I feel really bad about this joke, and that I am actually quite a fan of Andy Richter and all his failed sitcoms.

ELECTION DAY

Congratulations! You've made it to the finish line, Election Day. All that's left is the voting-booth photo op, after which you will hole up in your campaign headquarters and wait for the returns. Thanks to the miracle of exit polling, you'll know whether or not you've won long before the voting ceases.[1]

Get out the scorecard and make sure you've filled in your score for every challenge. Double-check the numbers. Double-check again. This is your political life we're talking about.

Now, total the number of electoral votes you've earned through our series of challenges.

If you've earned 270 or more votes, I'm pleased to tell you that you are the next pretend president of the United States! Having completed the challenges in this book so successfully, you're also very well prepared to take your hard-earned knowledge into the real arena.

If you have fewer than 200 electoral votes: I'm sorry, you've lost. Still, you'll be able to get good work (investigations, commissions, that kind of thing). Maybe even Commissioner of Baseball, if you're lucky.

---

[1] Right, President Kerry?

If you have between 200 and 269 electoral votes, you're in a hanging-chad situation, if you will, and therefore the race will be decided by the results of the challenges that are scored by me and my minions.[2] You'll have to wait for us to get back to you.

Either way, you've read an entire book, which is a feat in and of itself and something not everyone can claim. Feel good about that, loser.

---

[2] Okay, my minions.

ACKNOWLEDGMENTS

As always, thanks to Jane Friedman and everyone else at F+W Publications for their commitment to TOW Books.

Thanks to Annelise Robey for guiding me through the thornier parts of the publishing process.

Thanks to Mike Warner, my first and best reader for this book.

Thanks to Wikipedia for providing information that is just accurate enough.

Thanks to the following for past, present, and ongoing support: My family, Kevin Guilfoile, Dave Eggers, Chris Monks, Leo J. Shapiro & Associates, the Department of Communication at Virginia Tech.

Forever and always thanks to Kathy.

And of course thank you to the American politician for being the gift that never stops giving.

ABOUT THE AUTHOR

John Warner is the author of *Fondling Your Muse: Infallible Advice From a Published Author to the Writerly Aspirant* (a November 2005 BookSense pick), and (with Kevin Guilfoile) *My First Presidentiary: A Scrapbook of George W. Bush* (a *Washington Post* #1 bestseller). He is Chief Creative Czar of TOW Books and editor of McSweeney's Internet Tendency. He teaches writing at Clemson University.

SCORE CARD

POSTIVE ELECTORAL VOTES

❏❏❏❏❏❏❏❏❏❏❏❏❏❏❏❏❏❏❏❏❏❏❏❏❏❏❏❏❏❏ +25
❏❏❏❏❏❏❏❏❏❏❏❏❏❏❏❏❏❏❏❏❏❏❏❏❏❏❏❏❏❏ +50
❏❏❏❏❏❏❏❏❏❏❏❏❏❏❏❏❏❏❏❏❏❏❏❏❏❏❏❏❏❏ +75
❏❏❏❏❏❏❏❏❏❏❏❏❏❏❏❏❏❏❏❏❏❏❏❏❏❏❏❏❏❏ +100
❏❏❏❏❏❏❏❏❏❏❏❏❏❏❏❏❏❏❏❏❏❏❏❏❏❏❏❏❏❏ +125
❏❏❏❏❏❏❏❏❏❏❏❏❏❏❏❏❏❏❏❏❏❏❏❏❏❏❏❏❏❏ +150
❏❏❏❏❏❏❏❏❏❏❏❏❏❏❏❏❏❏❏❏❏❏❏❏❏❏❏❏❏❏ +175
❏❏❏❏❏❏❏❏❏❏❏❏❏❏❏❏❏❏❏❏❏❏❏❏❏❏❏❏❏❏ +200
❏❏❏❏❏❏❏❏❏❏❏❏❏❏❏❏❏❏❏❏❏❏❏❏❏❏❏❏❏❏ +225
❏❏❏❏❏❏❏❏❏❏❏❏❏❏❏❏❏❏❏❏❏❏❏❏❏❏❏❏❏❏ +250
❏❏❏❏❏❏❏❏❏❏❏❏❏❏❏❏❏❏❏❏❏❏❏❏❏❏❏❏❏❏ +275
❏❏❏❏❏❏❏❏❏❏❏❏❏❏❏❏❏❏❏❏❏❏❏❏❏❏❏❏❏❏ +300

NEGATIVE ELECTORAL VOTES

❏❏❏❏❏❏❏❏❏❏❏❏❏❏❏❏❏❏❏❏❏❏❏❏❏❏❏❏❏❏ -25
❏❏❏❏❏❏❏❏❏❏❏❏❏❏❏❏❏❏❏❏❏❏❏❏❏❏❏❏❏❏ -50
❏❏❏❏❏❏❏❏❏❏❏❏❏❏❏❏❏❏❏❏❏❏❏❏❏❏❏❏❏❏ -75
❏❏❏❏❏❏❏❏❏❏❏❏❏❏❏❏❏❏❏❏❏❏❏❏❏❏❏❏❏❏ -100
❏❏❏❏❏❏❏❏❏❏❏❏❏❏❏❏❏❏❏❏❏❏❏❏❏❏❏❏❏❏ -125
❏❏❏❏❏❏❏❏❏❏❏❏❏❏❏❏❏❏❏❏❏❏❏❏❏❏❏❏❏❏ -150
❏❏❏❏❏❏❏❏❏❏❏❏❏❏❏❏❏❏❏❏❏❏❏❏❏❏❏❏❏❏ -175
❏❏❏❏❏❏❏❏❏❏❏❏❏❏❏❏❏❏❏❏❏❏❏❏❏❏❏❏❏❏ -200
❏❏❏❏❏❏❏❏❏❏❏❏❏❏❏❏❏❏❏❏❏❏❏❏❏❏❏❏❏❏ -225
❏❏❏❏❏❏❏❏❏❏❏❏❏❏❏❏❏❏❏❏❏❏❏❏❏❏❏❏❏❏ -250
❏❏❏❏❏❏❏❏❏❏❏❏❏❏❏❏❏❏❏❏❏❏❏❏❏❏❏❏❏❏ -275
❏❏❏❏❏❏❏❏❏❏❏❏❏❏❏❏❏❏❏❏❏❏❏❏❏❏❏❏❏❏ -300

TOTAL: _____